The Apprenticeship of
ANDREW WYETH
Painting a Family Legacy

GENE BARRETTA

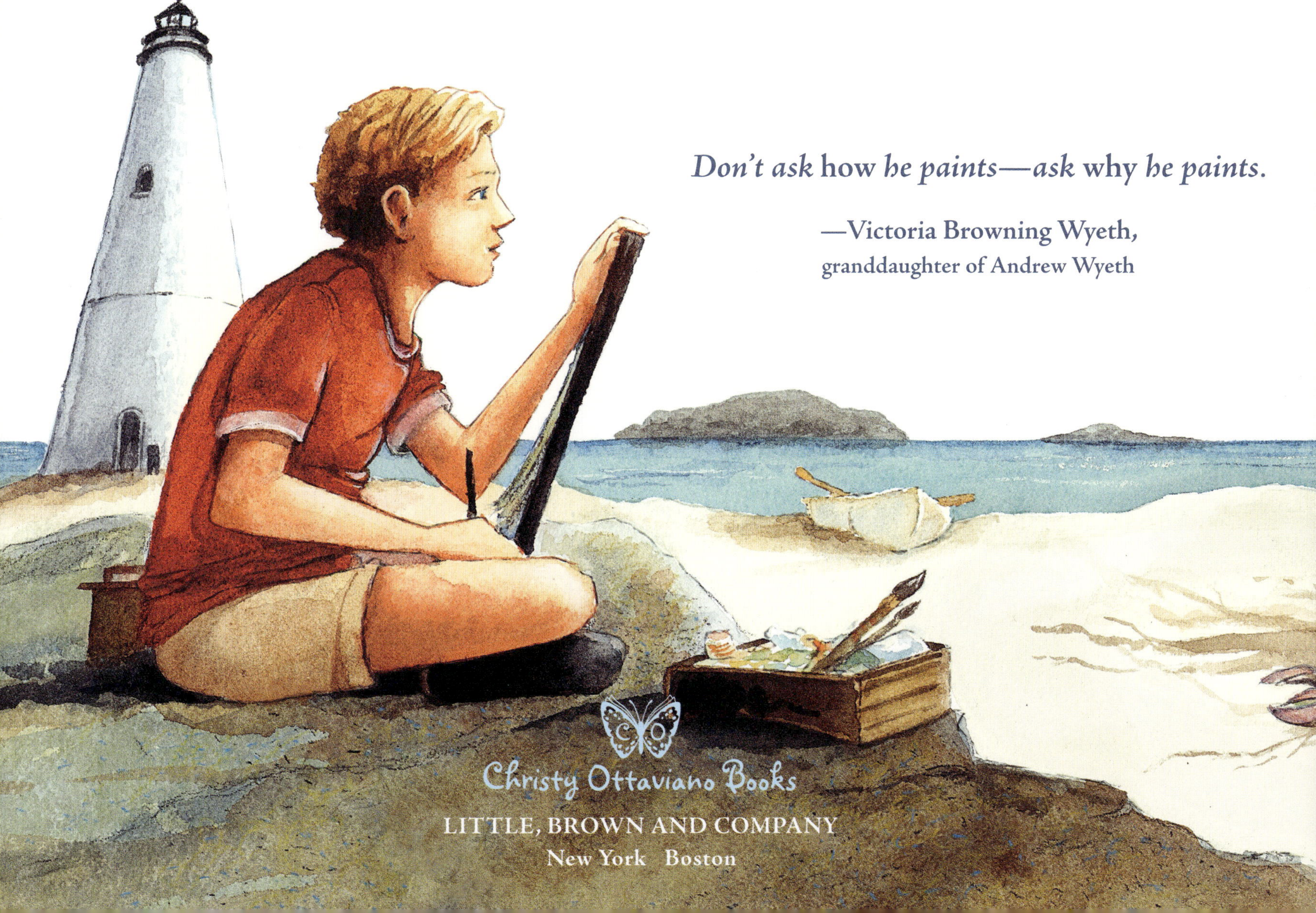

Don't ask how he paints—ask why he paints.

—Victoria Browning Wyeth,
granddaughter of Andrew Wyeth

Christy Ottaviano Books

LITTLE, BROWN AND COMPANY
New York Boston

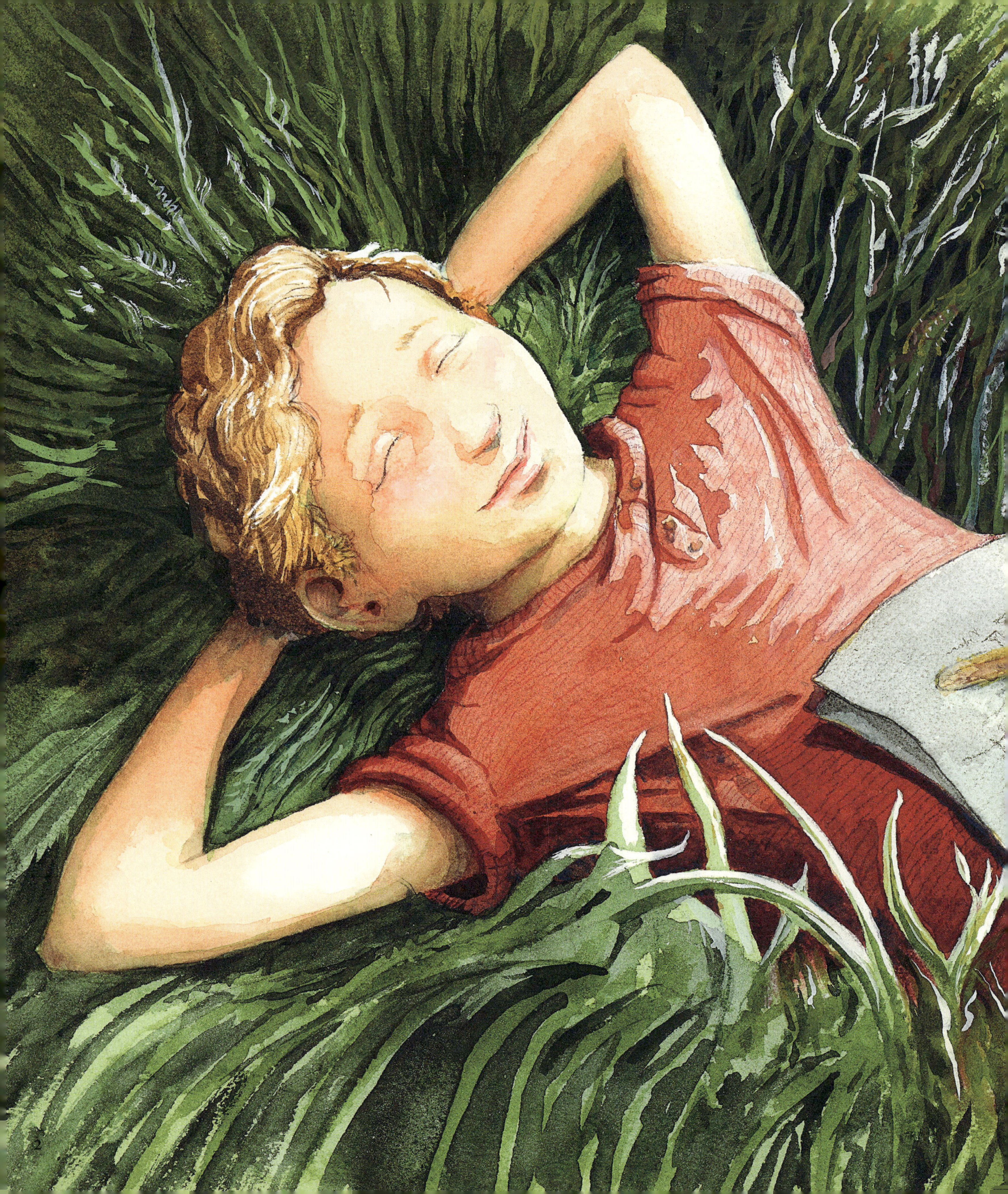

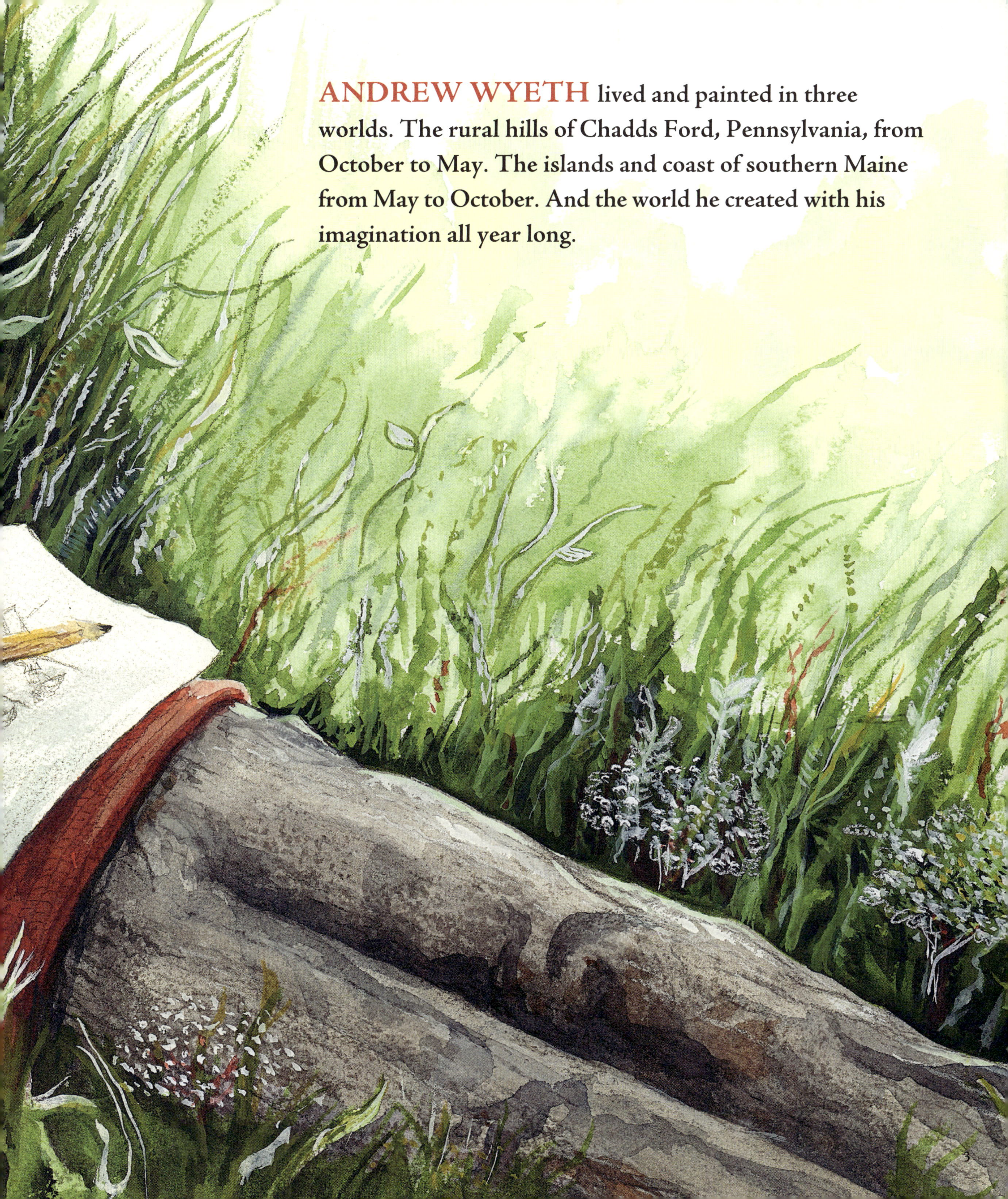

ANDREW WYETH lived and painted in three worlds. The rural hills of Chadds Ford, Pennsylvania, from October to May. The islands and coast of southern Maine from May to October. And the world he created with his imagination all year long.

It was the most inspiring childhood a boy like Andy could want.

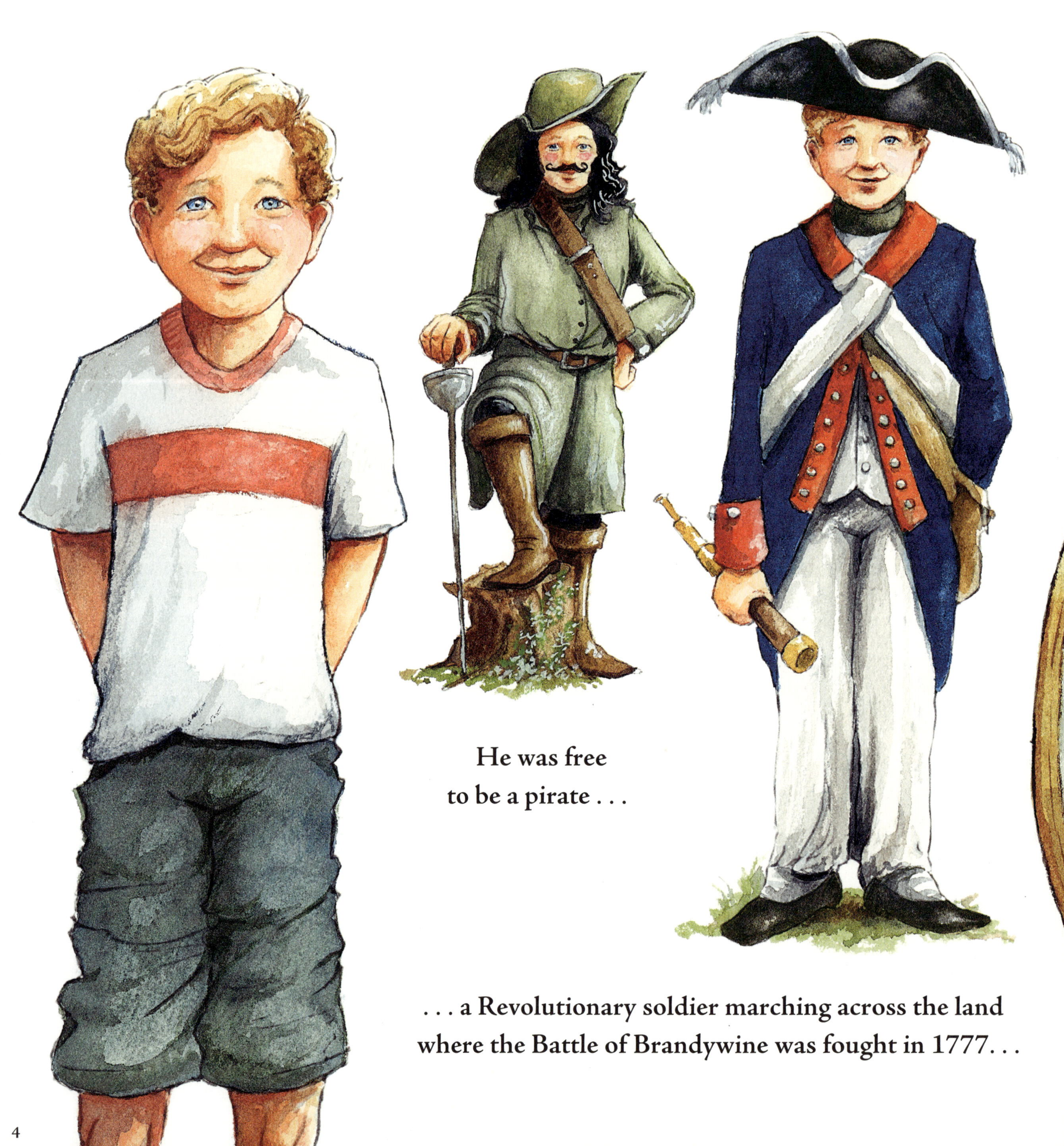

He was free
to be a pirate . . .

. . . a Revolutionary soldier marching across the land
where the Battle of Brandywine was fought in 1777 . . .

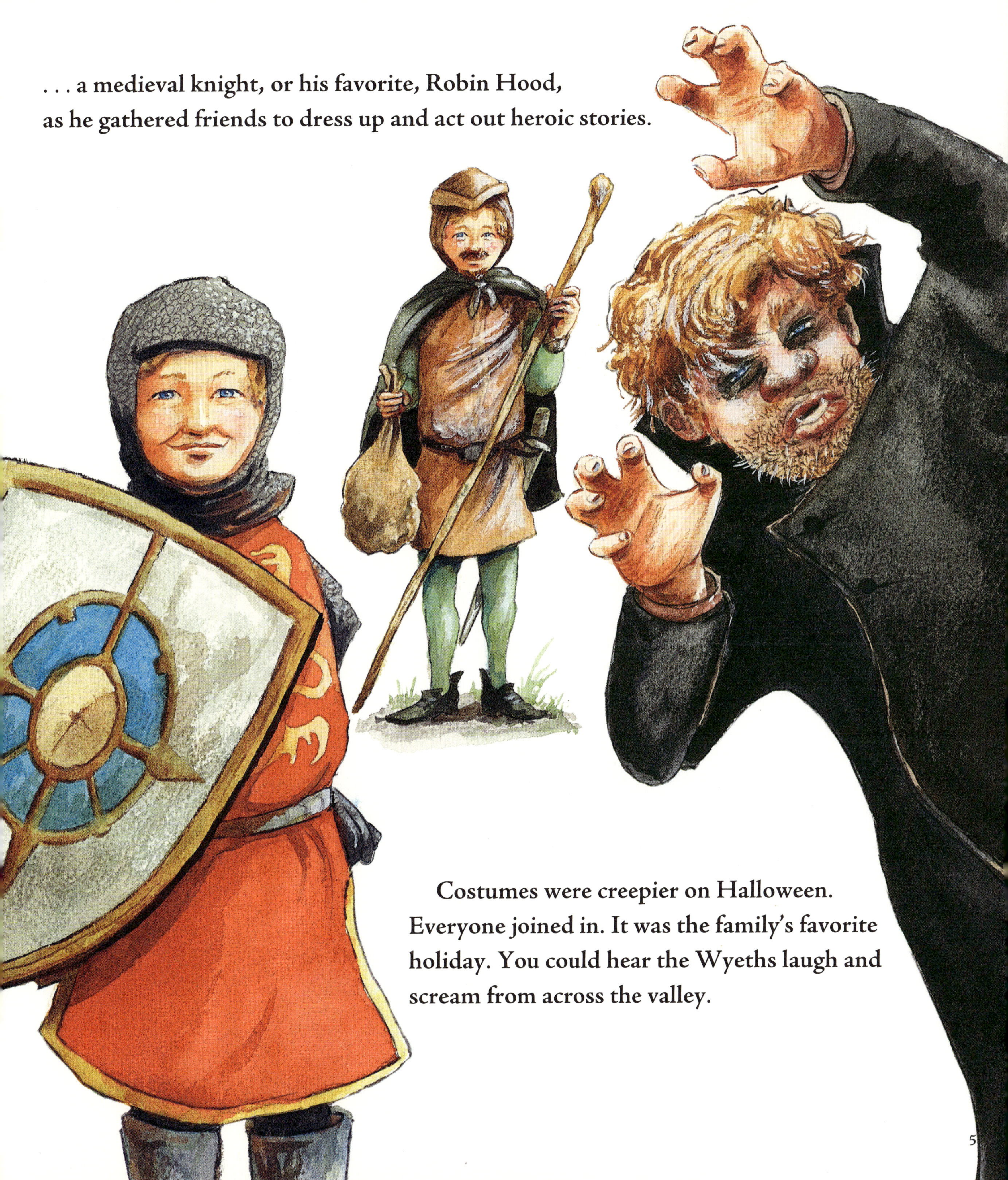

. . . a medieval knight, or his favorite, Robin Hood,
as he gathered friends to dress up and act out heroic stories.

Costumes were creepier on Halloween.
Everyone joined in. It was the family's favorite
holiday. You could hear the Wyeths laugh and
scream from across the valley.

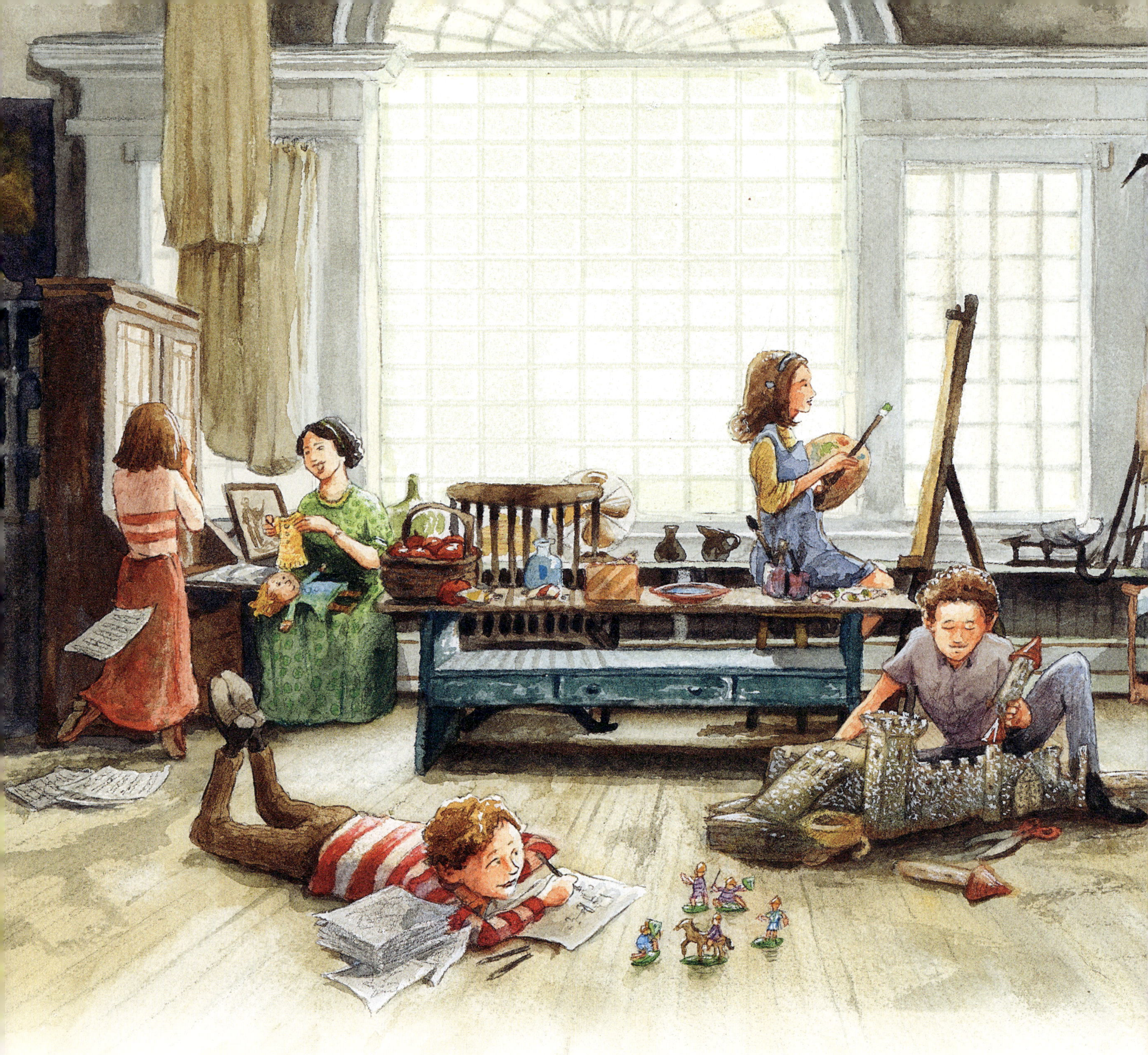

Andy's father used the same costumes for his paintings. His name, N.C. Wyeth, was recognized throughout the country as one of the premier storybook illustrators. At home, he was simply Pa.

The studio door was always open, because N.C. was eager to raise a new generation of artists. His children watched as his illustrations evolved from pencil scribbles to lively adventures that leaped off the canvas.

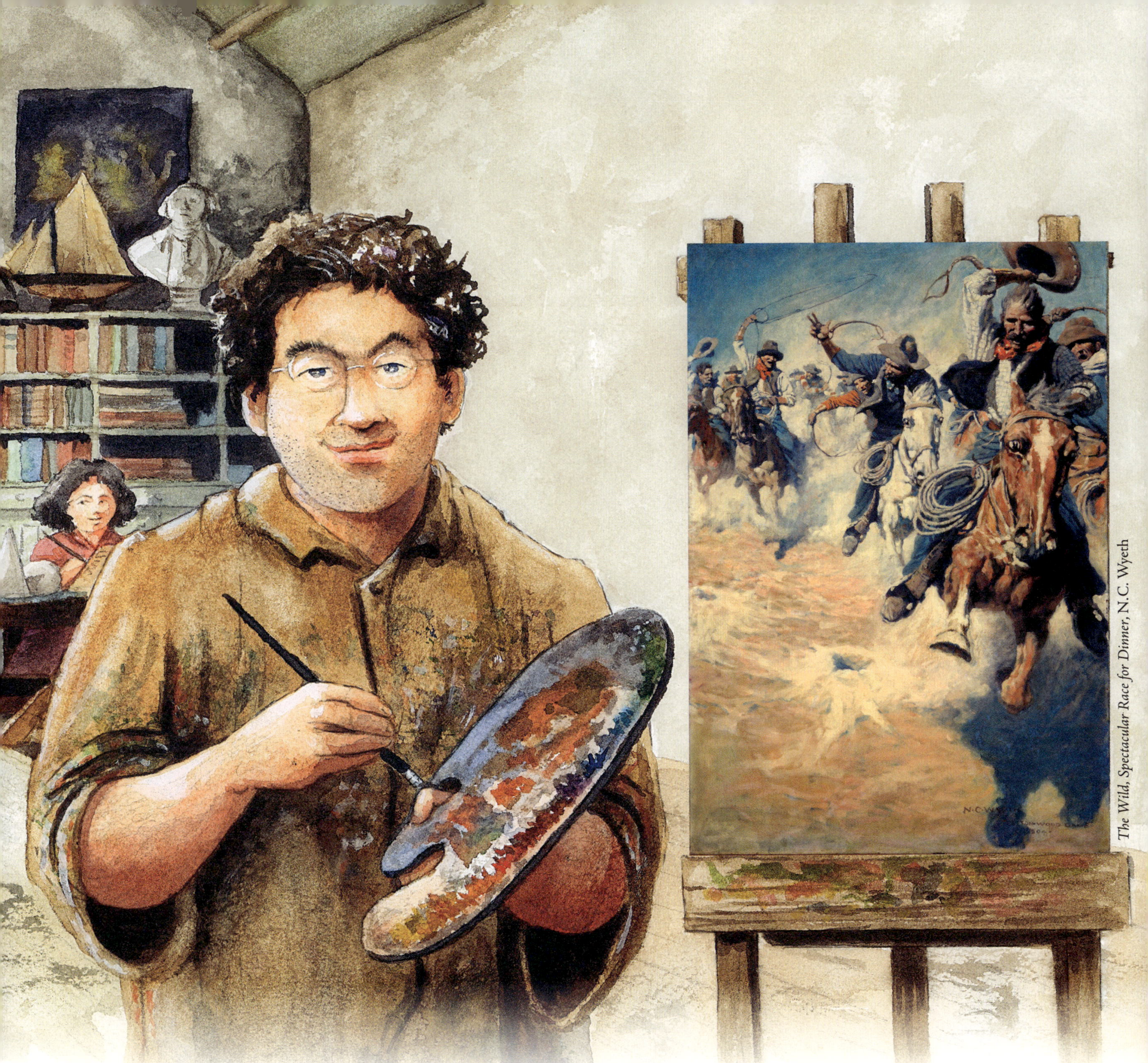

Pa was a giant in their eyes. His larger-than-life personality and passion were contagious. By the time Andy was six, all he wanted to do was draw.

Each of the Wyeth children were creative. In their home, there was no other way to be. Henriette and Carolyn loved to paint. Nathaniel built elaborate handmade models. Ann filled the air with piano music. Even Ma would pitch in to sew clothes for Ann's dolls.

Art was a comfort for Andy, especially because his health was frail due to serious hip and lung issues. He was taught at home by a tutor, but most of the day was spent alone, drawing, playing with toy soldiers, and exploring every inch of the local fields and creeks.

David Lawrence, his best friend in Chadds Ford, introduced him to a neighborhood he would paint his entire life. The people fascinated him. Their stories were rich, and their homes looked as though they had grown out of the ground like their gardens and crops. Andy fit right in. It was not unusual to find him sitting nearby, quietly observing and sketching.

He painted vultures circling above, farmer Karl Kuerner leading a parade of cows into his barn, and a somber yet spirited funeral service at Mother Archie's Church.

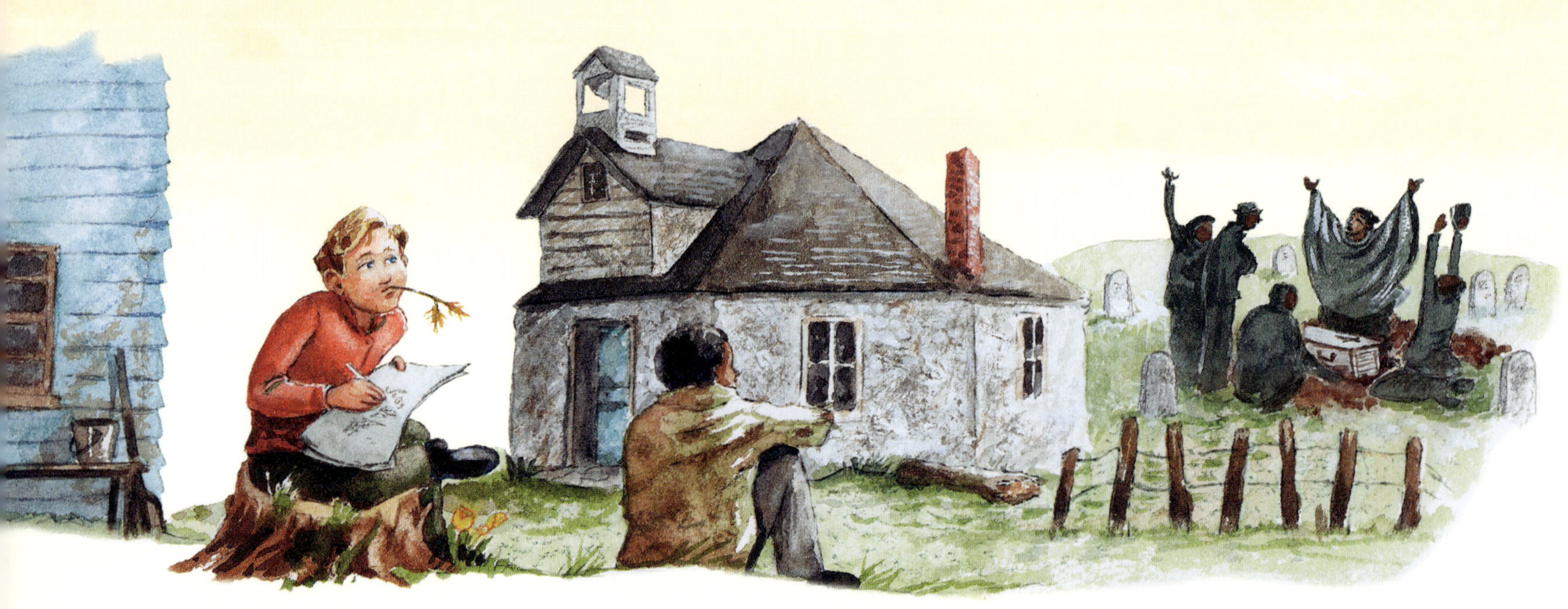

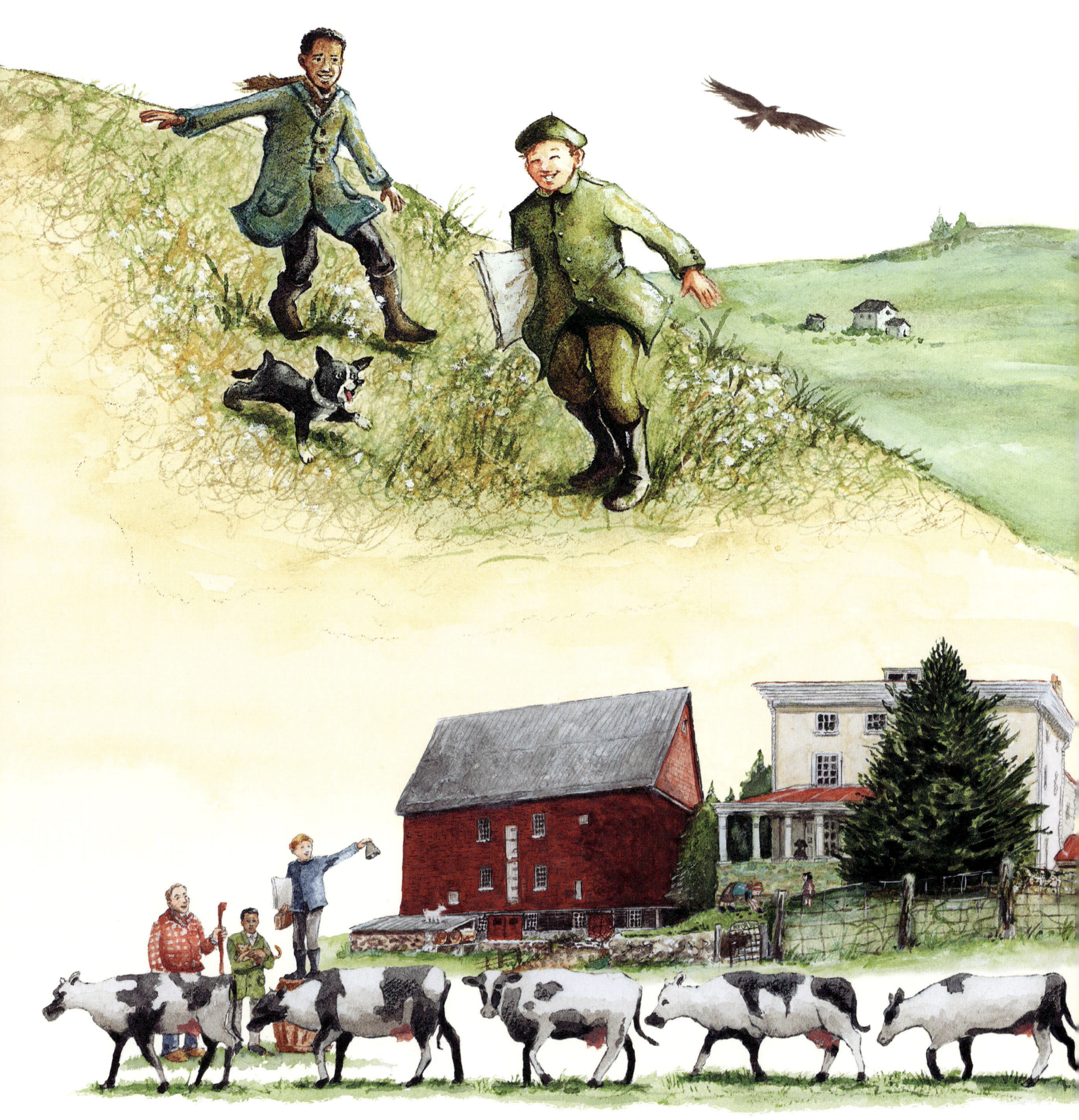

October 19, 1932, was an exciting day in Chadds Ford.

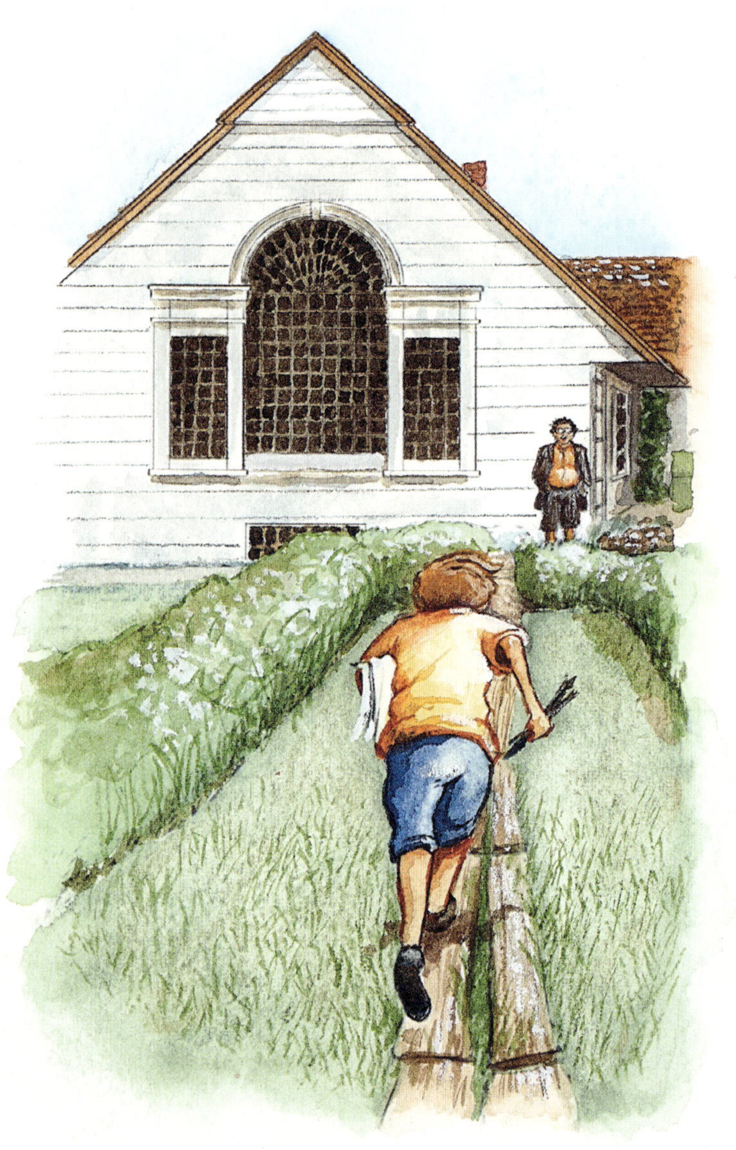
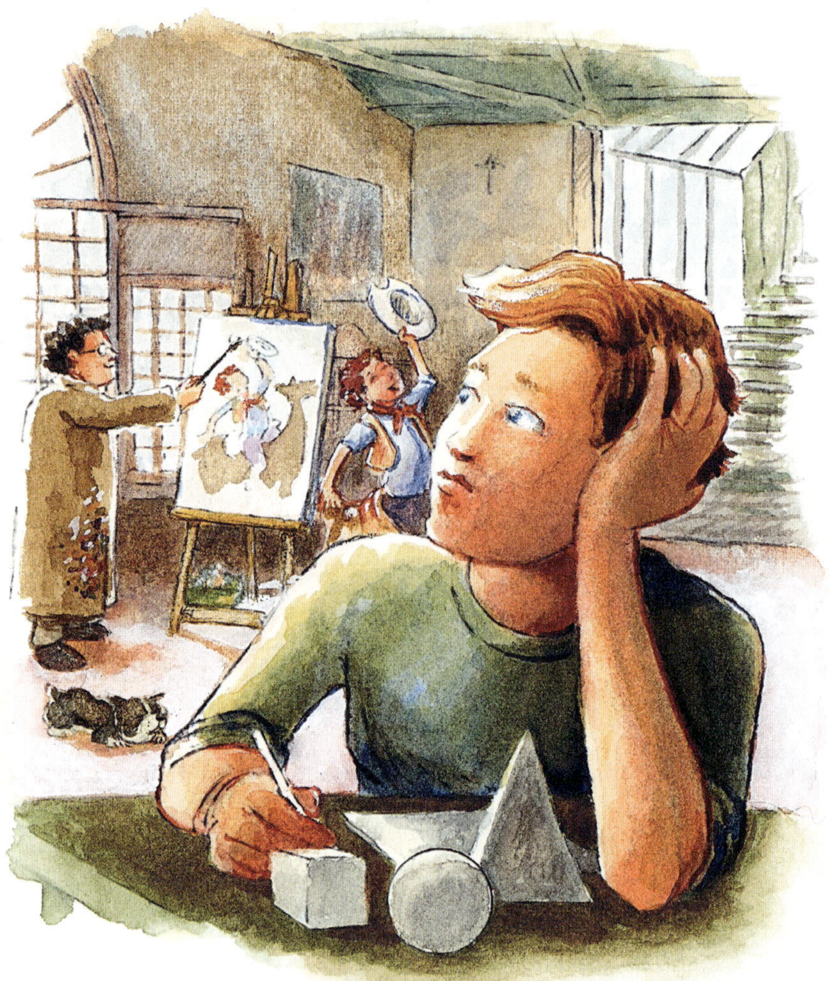

Fifteen-year-old Andy entered Pa's studio as an official apprentice, eager to start painting swashbuckling pirates and brave knights on horseback!

Pa had different plans: Start with the basics. Draw simple shapes over and over to study light and shadow. After that, draw live models to study the human body.

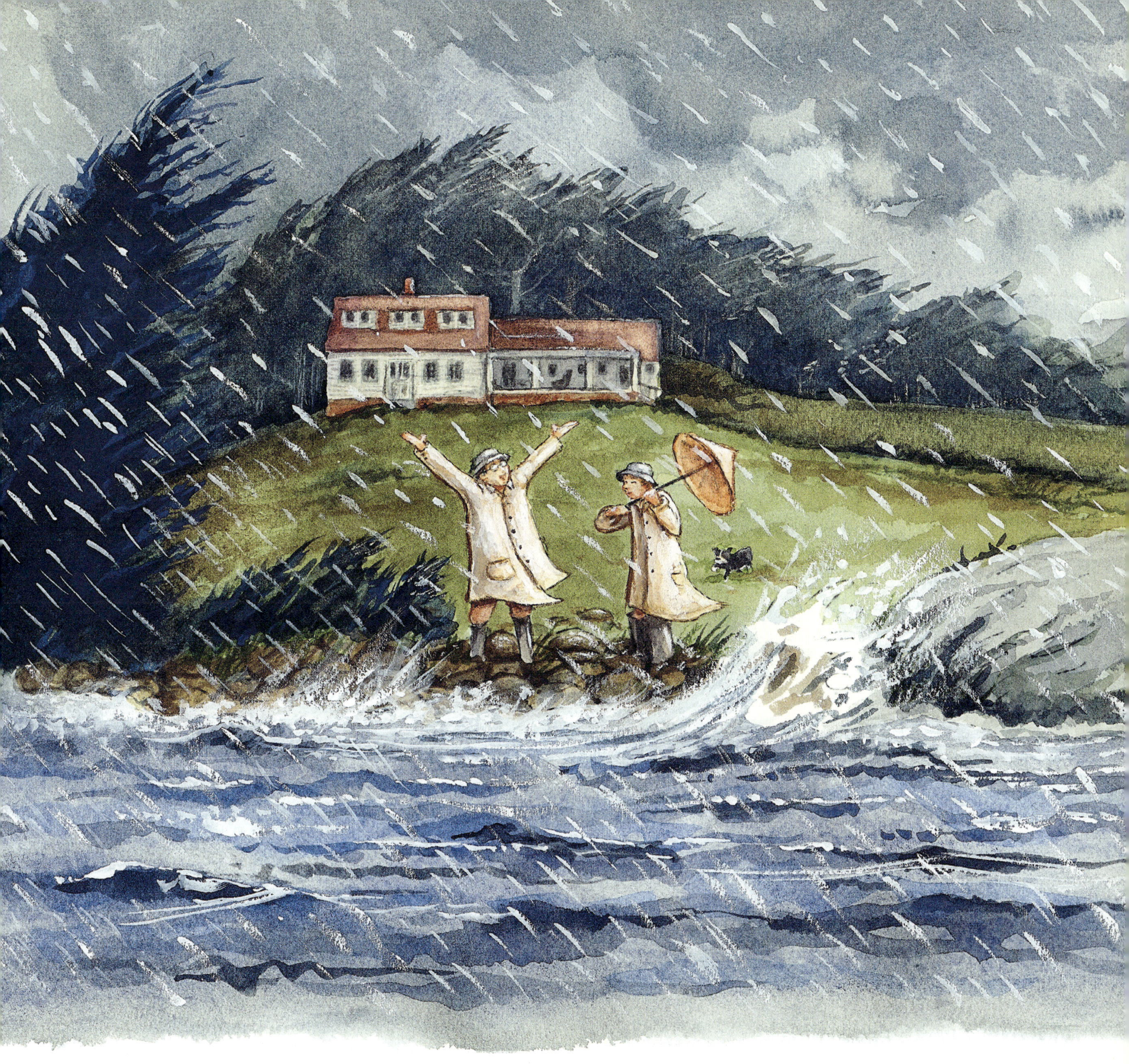

During long walks, Andy was taught to love every detail in nature and see the world like an artist. "Andy, you know, we must be like a sponge," Pa said. "Soak it all up. But be sure you squeeze some out every once in a while."

In Maine, Andy could name the type of bird silhouetted high in the clouds and tell the time of day by the length of the lighthouse shadows.

Everything felt alive and full of personality. He wondered what the trees had seen during their long lives. Did birds feel heavy on their branches? Could their leaves sense an approaching storm?

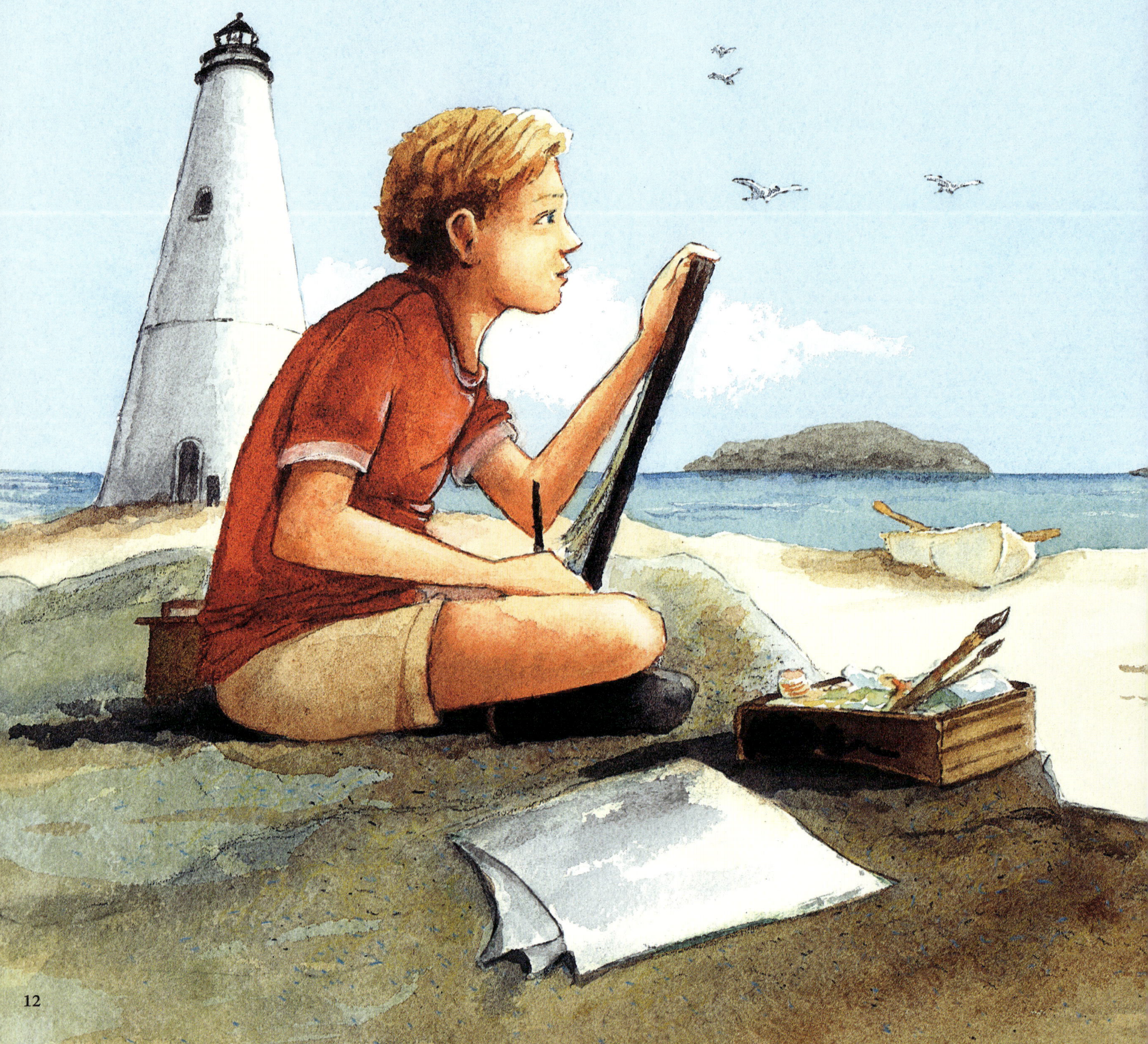

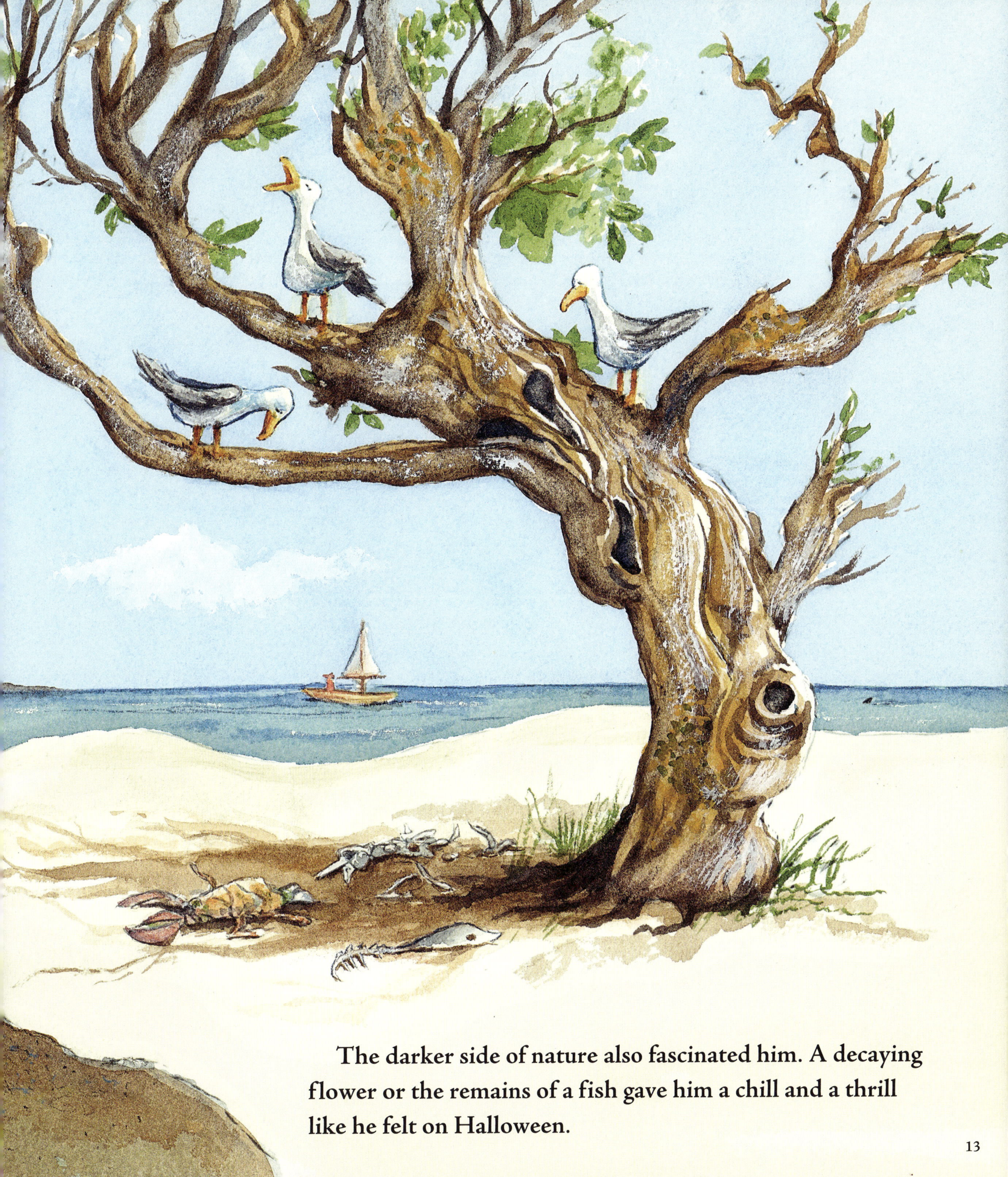

The darker side of nature also fascinated him. A decaying
flower or the remains of a fish gave him a chill and a thrill
like he felt on Halloween.

His talent was remarkable for someone so young. Still, Pa could be bossy about *what* to paint and *how* to paint it.

Andy never forgot the day he shared a painting of his friend Bill Loper, who had lost his left hand in an accident and replaced it with a hook. Without hesitation, Pa decided the hook was wrong for the painting and wiped it off the canvas.

Andy was crushed. That was *his* painting! He wanted to paint it the way *he* saw it.

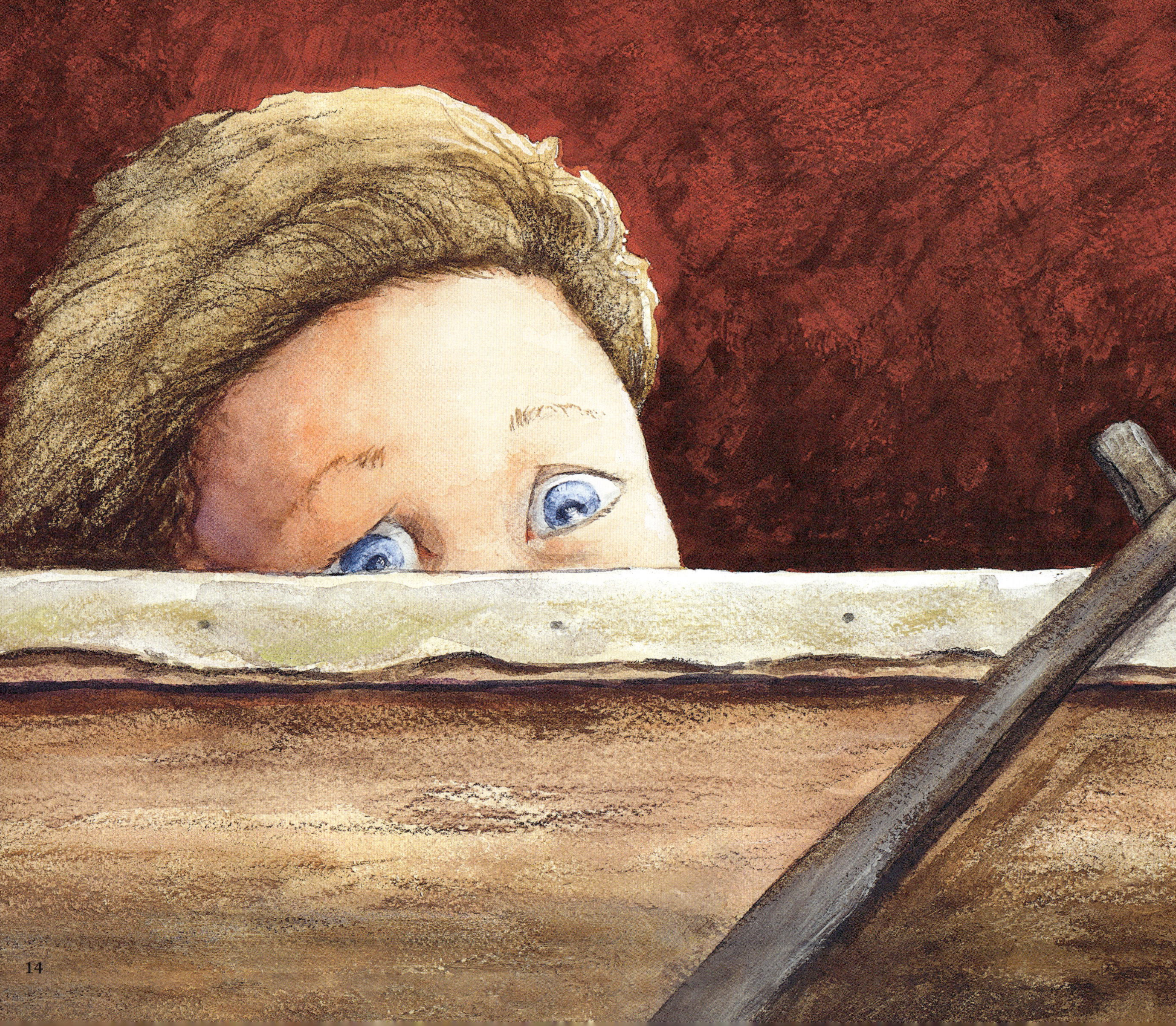

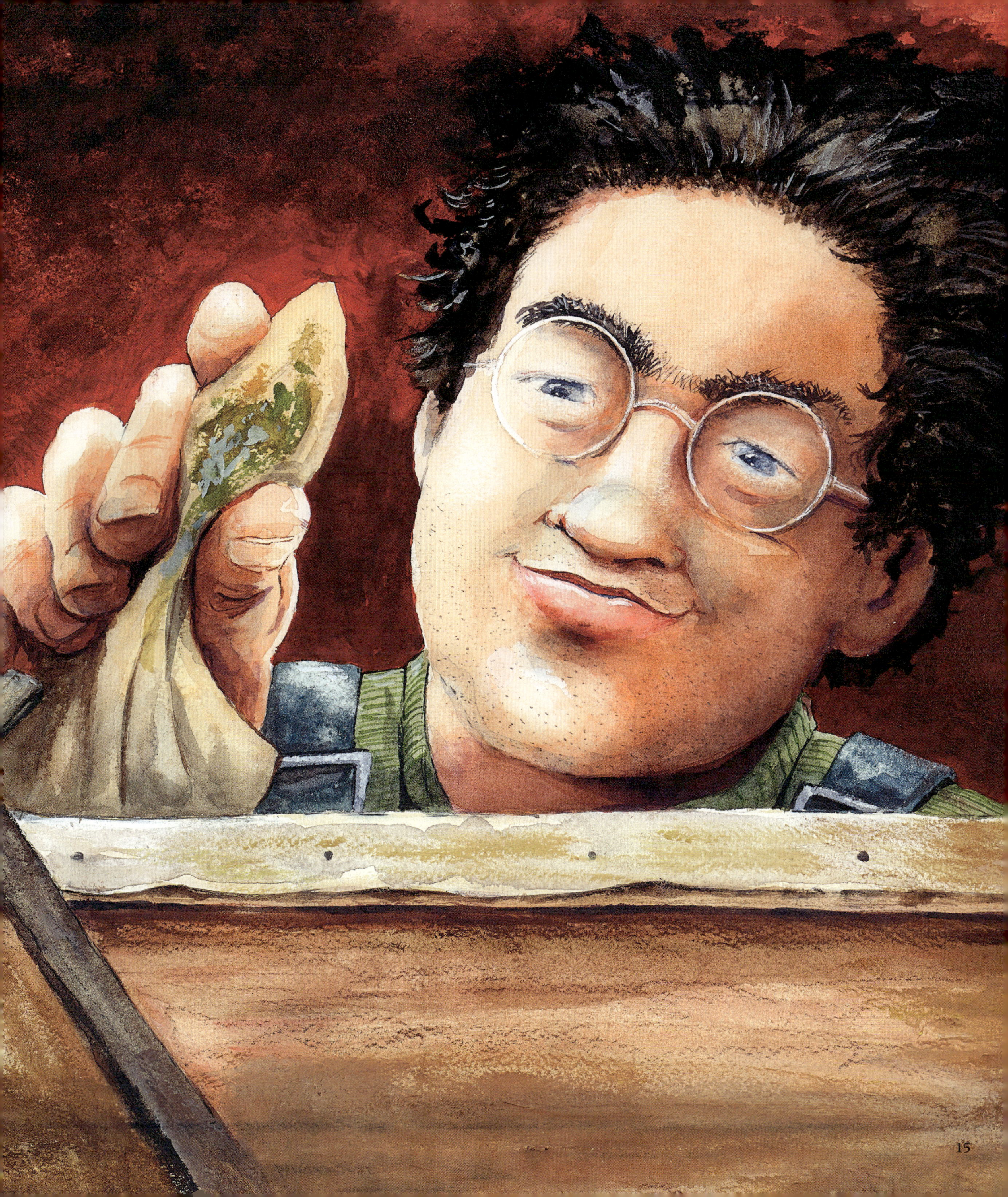

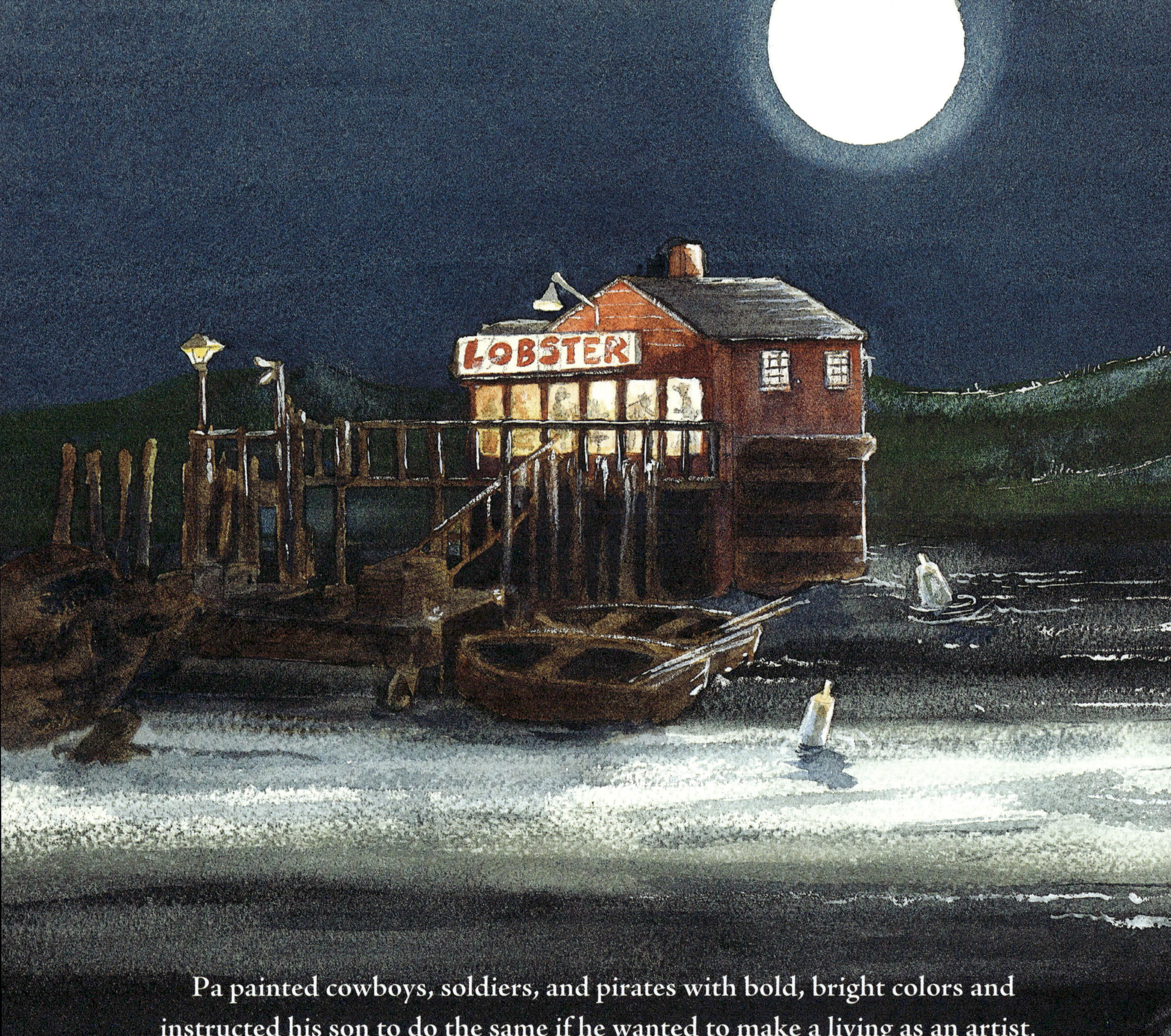

Pa painted cowboys, soldiers, and pirates with bold, bright colors and instructed his son to do the same if he wanted to make a living as an artist. In Andy's mind, the most exciting characters, places, and stories to paint were the ones he lived with every day. Like his best friend in Maine, Walt Anderson, as they rowed around the islands getting into trouble and taking lobster from the fishermen's traps. Walt was his pirate.

After a few years, Andy had created enough work to join Pa, Henriette, and Carolyn in family art shows.

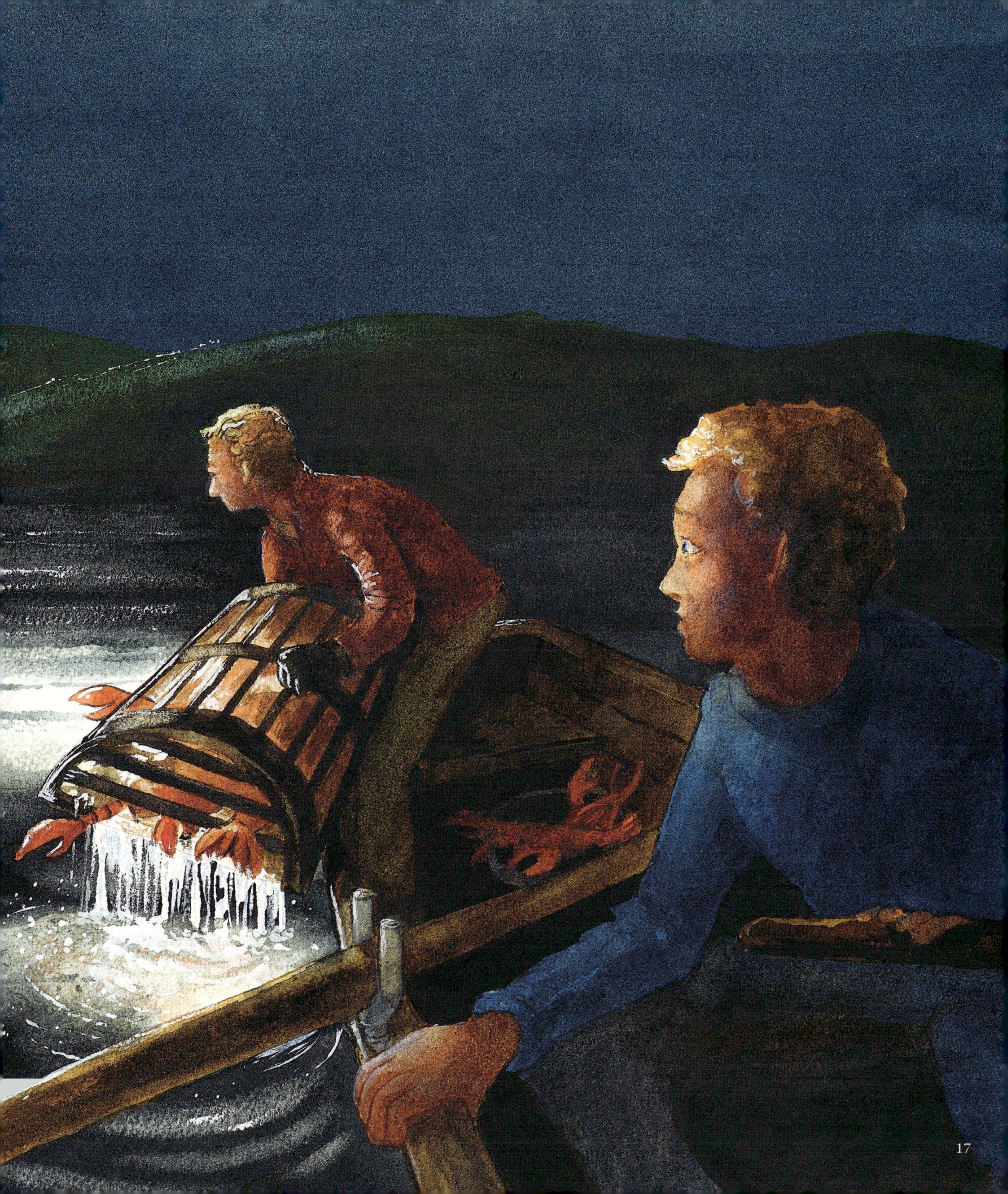

October 19 would once again be a memorable date in Andy's life.
New York City, 1937. Opening night.

When he was only twenty years old, the renowned Macbeth Gallery in New
York City agreed to host a solo show of his work. Andy was excited but nervous.
Would strangers love his paintings as much as his family and friends did?

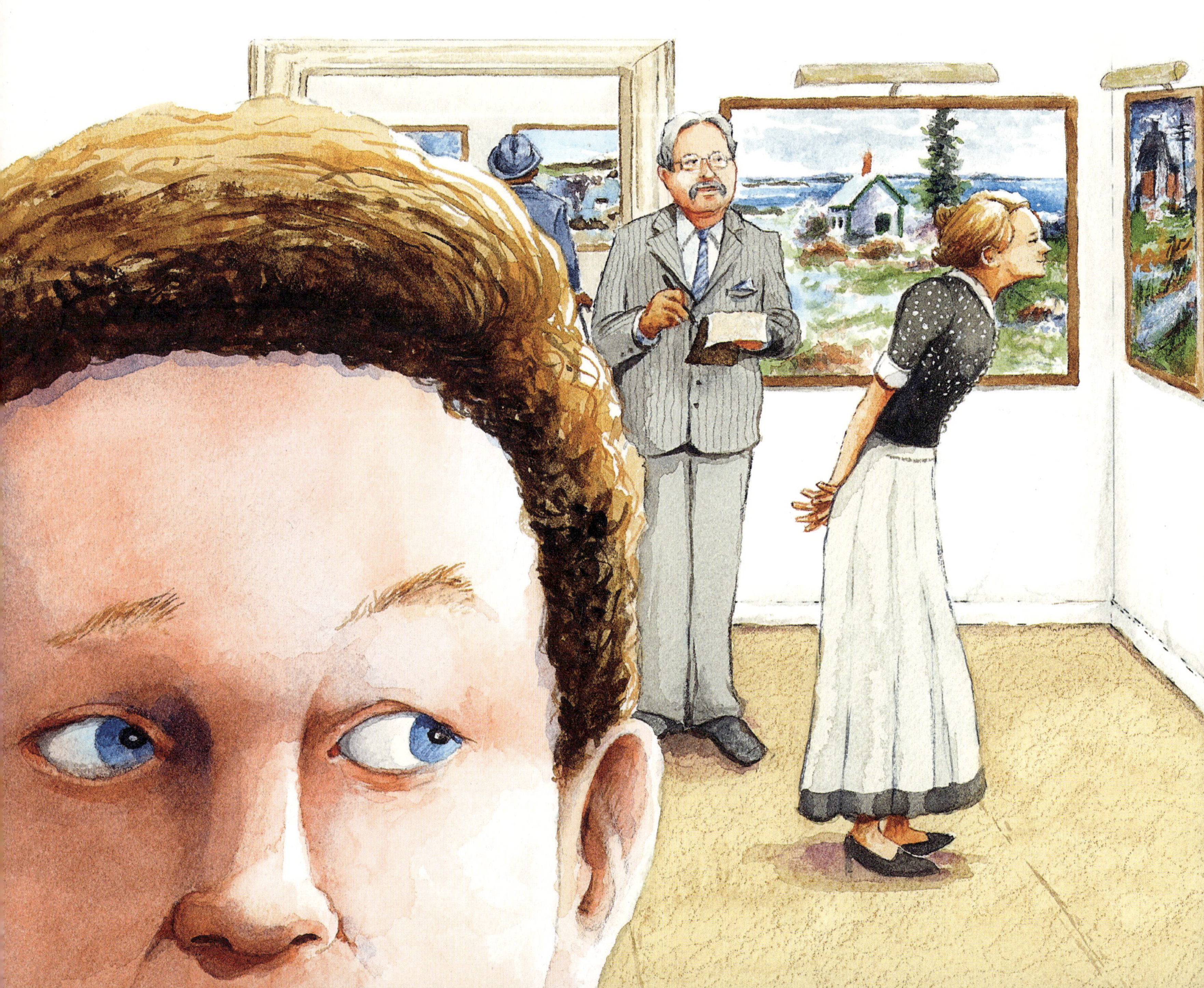

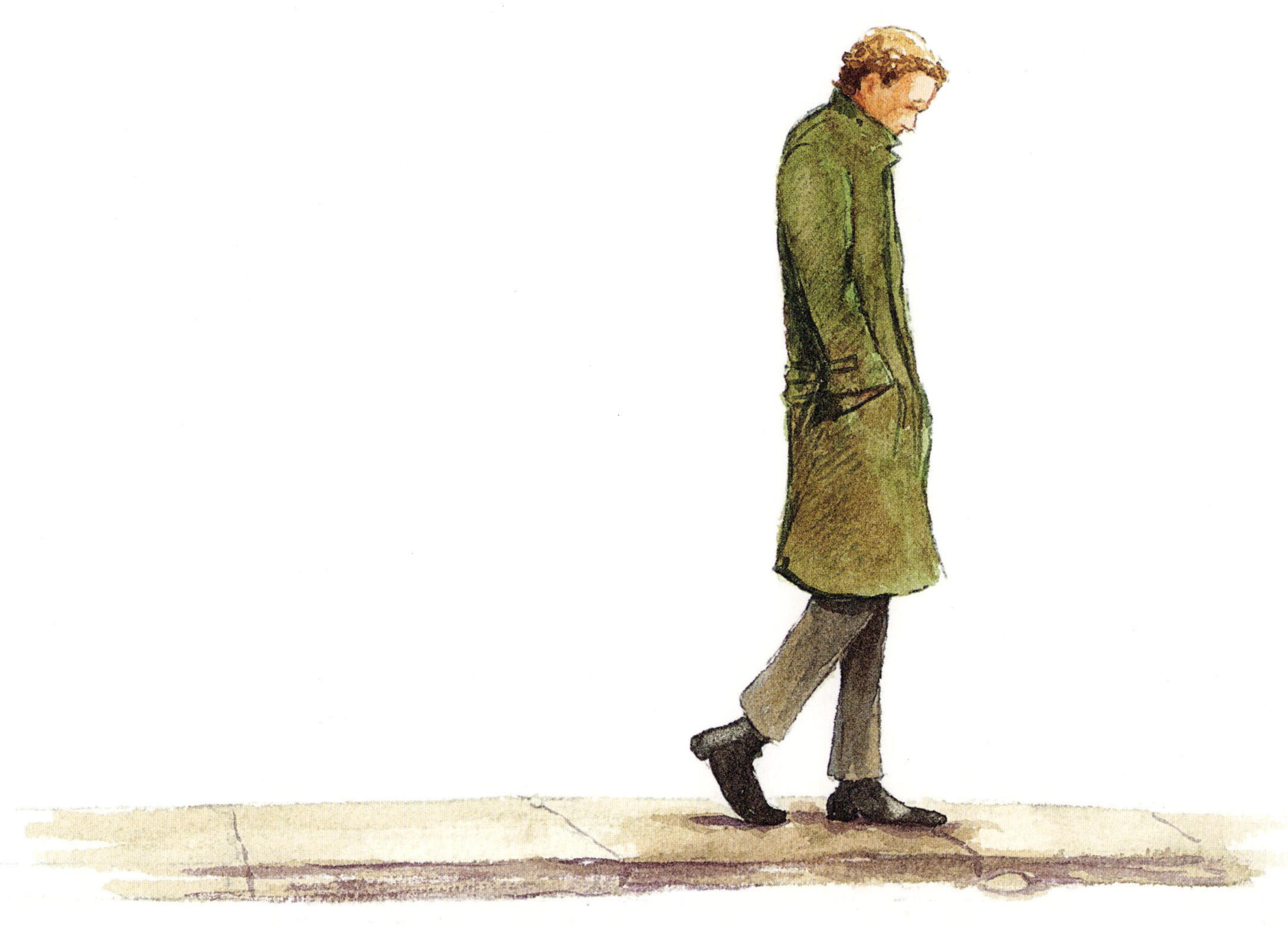

When the gallery closed on opening night, he had his answer. Only one painting had sold. Sure, he knew it was his first New York show. He also knew not to get his hopes up. But what he didn't realize was that exciting news was already spreading throughout the art community.

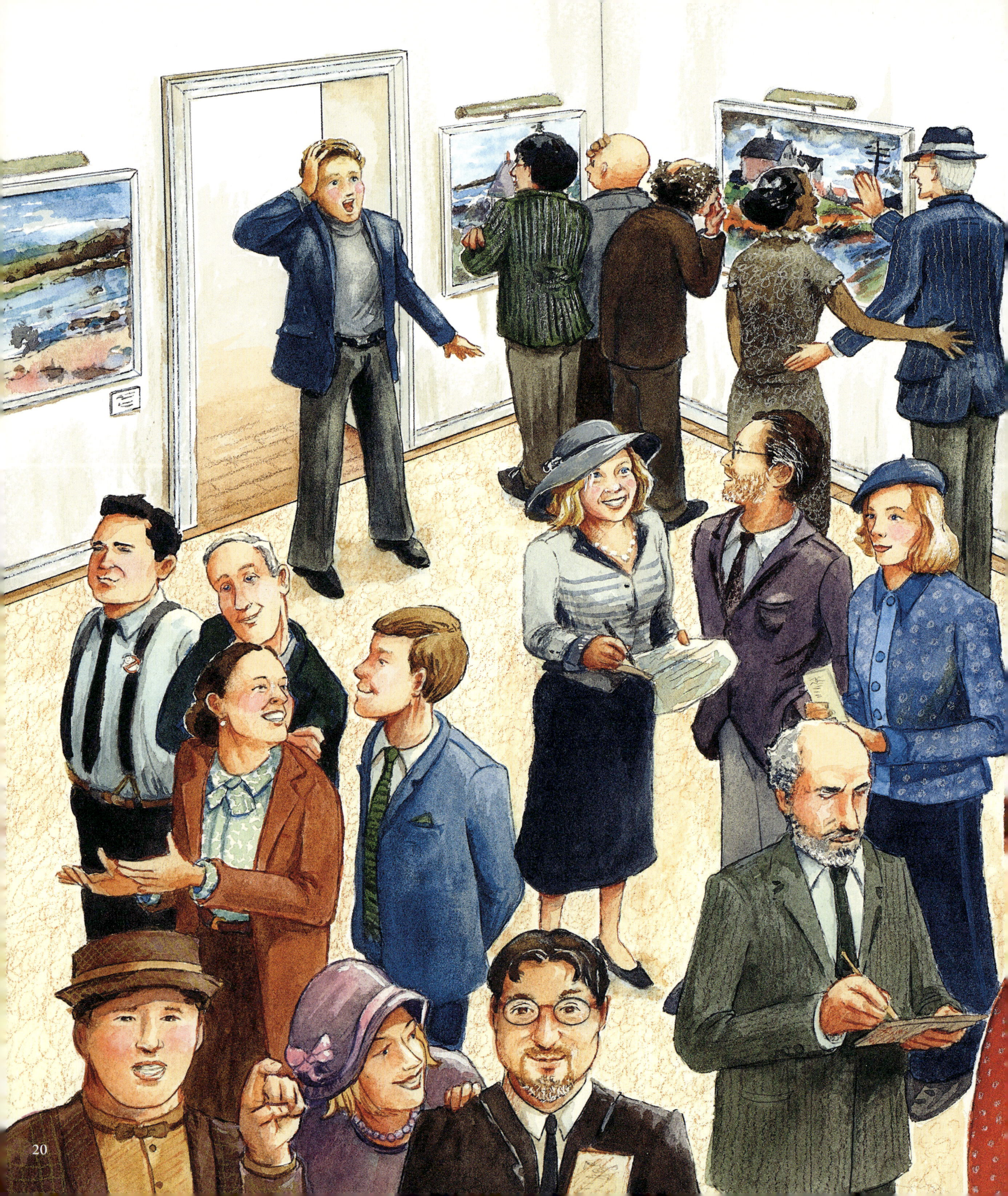

The next day, when Andy stepped into the gallery, he almost fainted. All twenty-three paintings had sold! The rooms were filled with art collectors, critics, and museum owners. One art dealer declared, "At last, a man who has the guts to present nature honestly, powerfully, and beautifully." Now Andy had everyone's attention.

There were more shows, and more paintings sold. Yet there was something he wanted more than all that—the freedom to paint without Pa looking over his shoulder. He loved Pa's work, but he didn't want to paint like Pa.

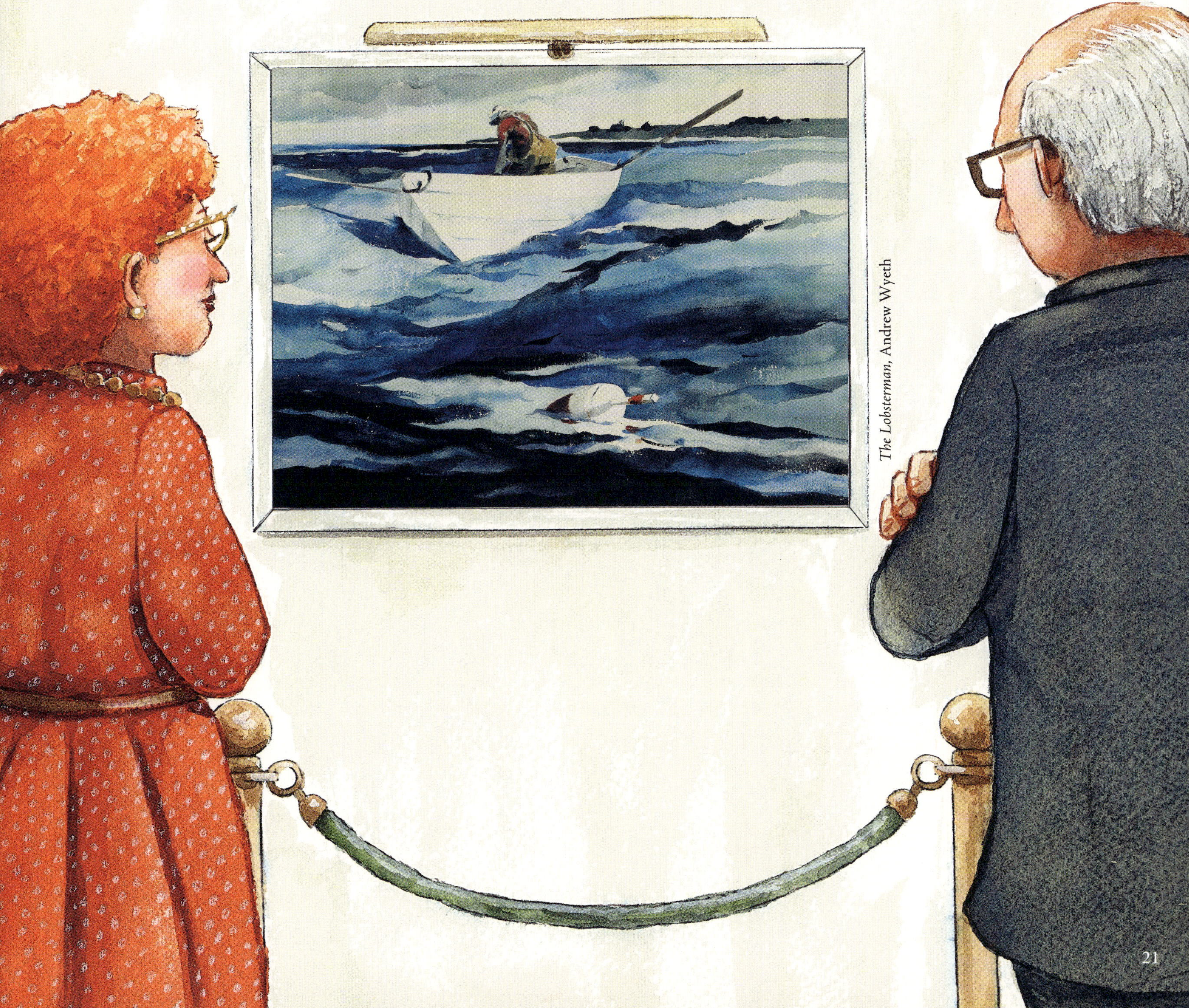

Fortunately, there was Betsy James. On Andy's twenty-second birthday, they met at her family home in Cushing, Maine. Betsy remembers, "I knew at some point somebody was going to find me and know what I was all about." Before meeting Andy, she had never heard anyone speak about sunlight crossing the floor or how fields change color with the seasons. Andy felt a similar connection.

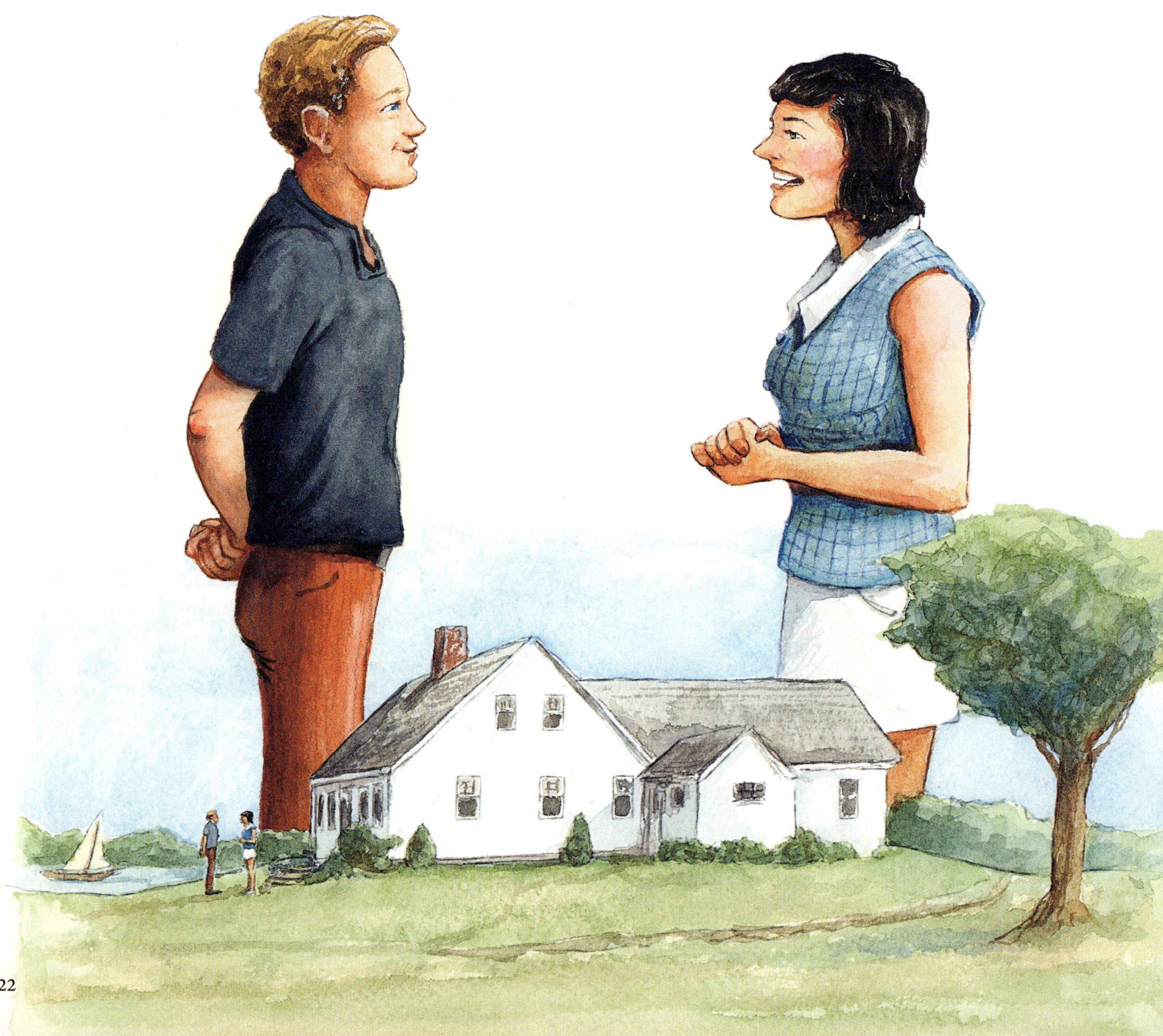

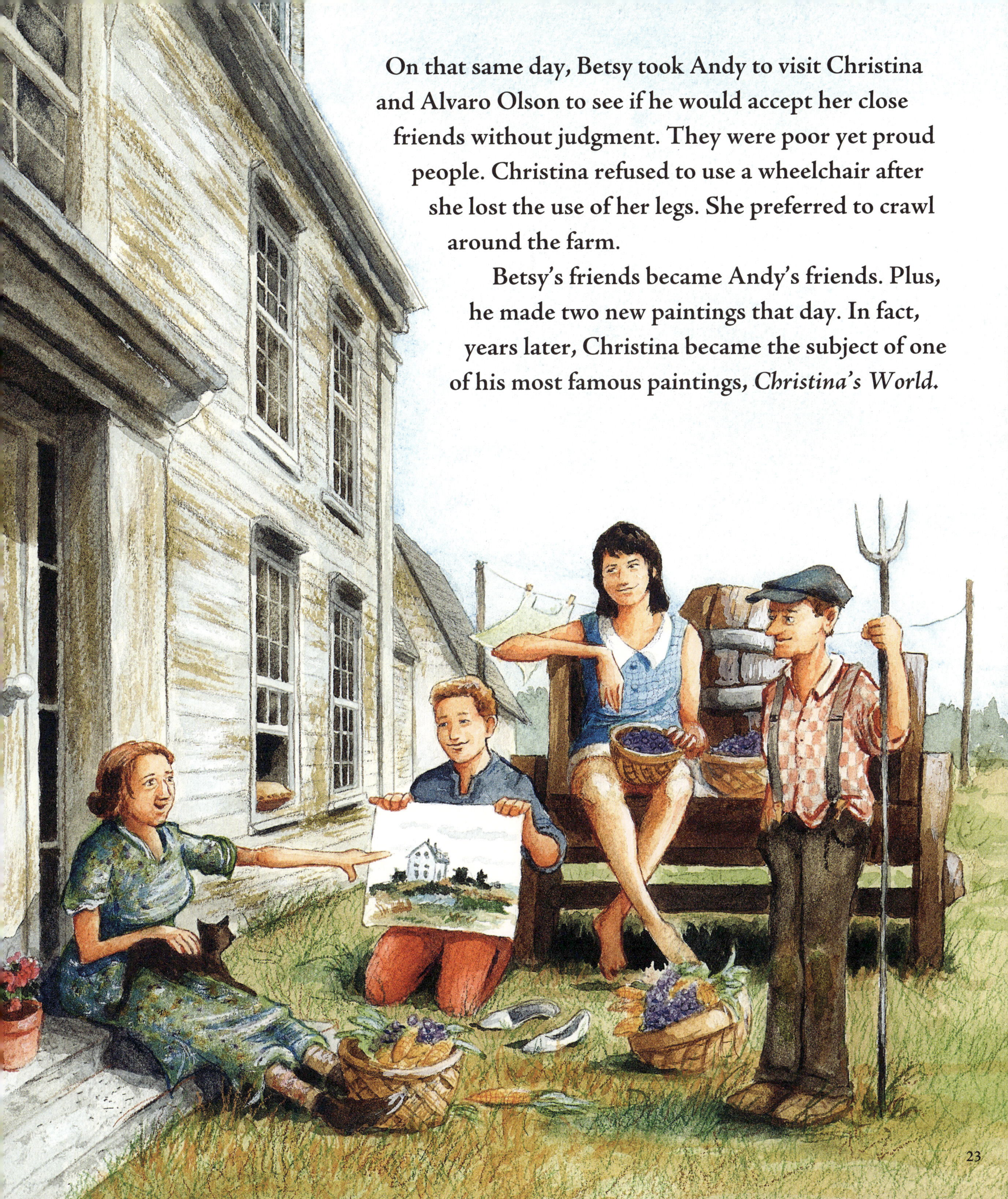

On that same day, Betsy took Andy to visit Christina and Alvaro Olson to see if he would accept her close friends without judgment. They were poor yet proud people. Christina refused to use a wheelchair after she lost the use of her legs. She preferred to crawl around the farm.

Betsy's friends became Andy's friends. Plus, he made two new paintings that day. In fact, years later, Christina became the subject of one of his most famous paintings, *Christina's World.*

Love grew quickly. The young couple saw each other as much as possible. Betsy insisted that Andy paint only for himself. She also encouraged him to continue painting in a new medium he loved called egg tempera, made from water, color pigment powder, and egg yolk.

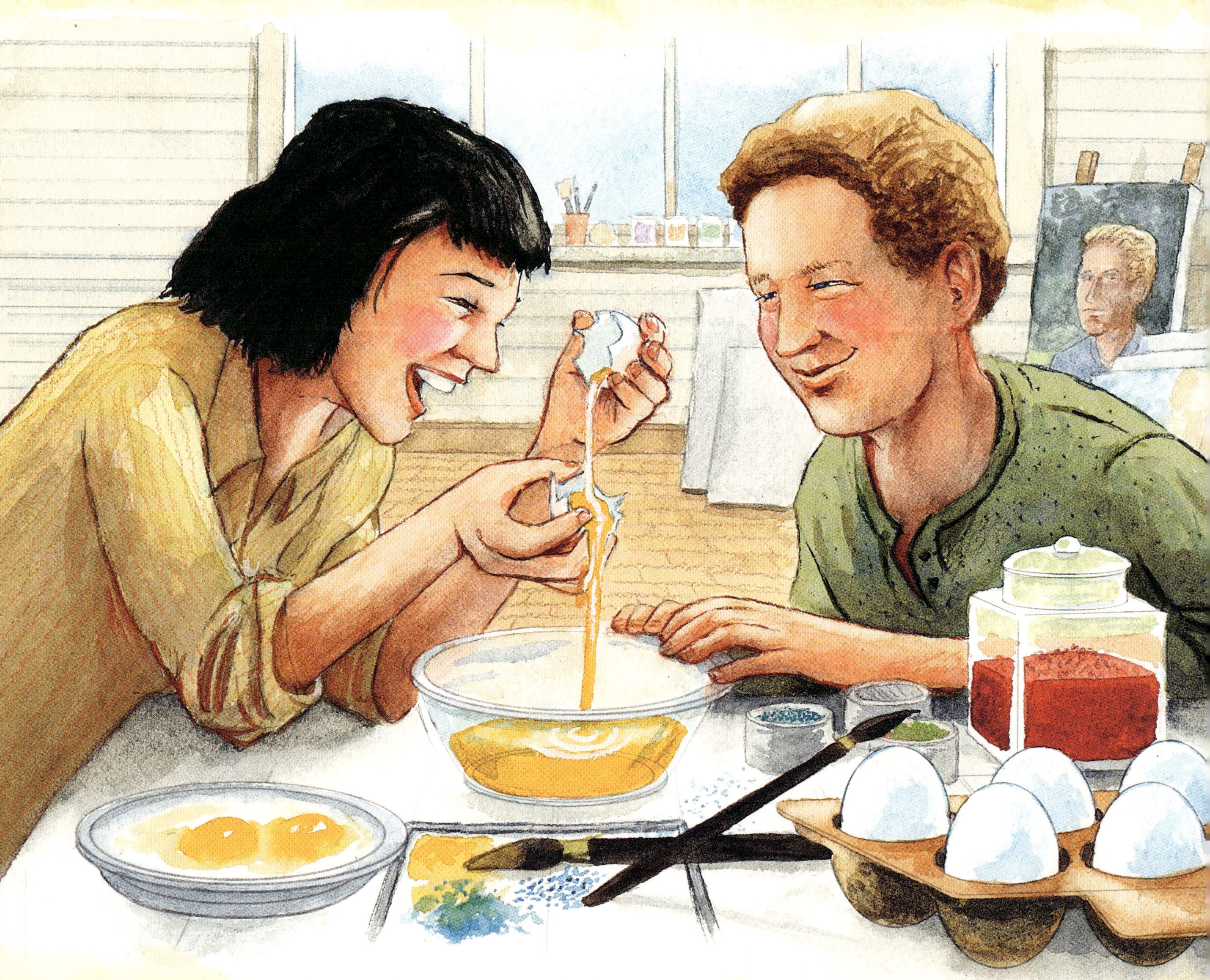

One evening, Andy confessed to Pa that he couldn't focus on painting because he was so deeply in love. "Well, then you better marry her," Pa replied. Andy and Betsy were married within a year.

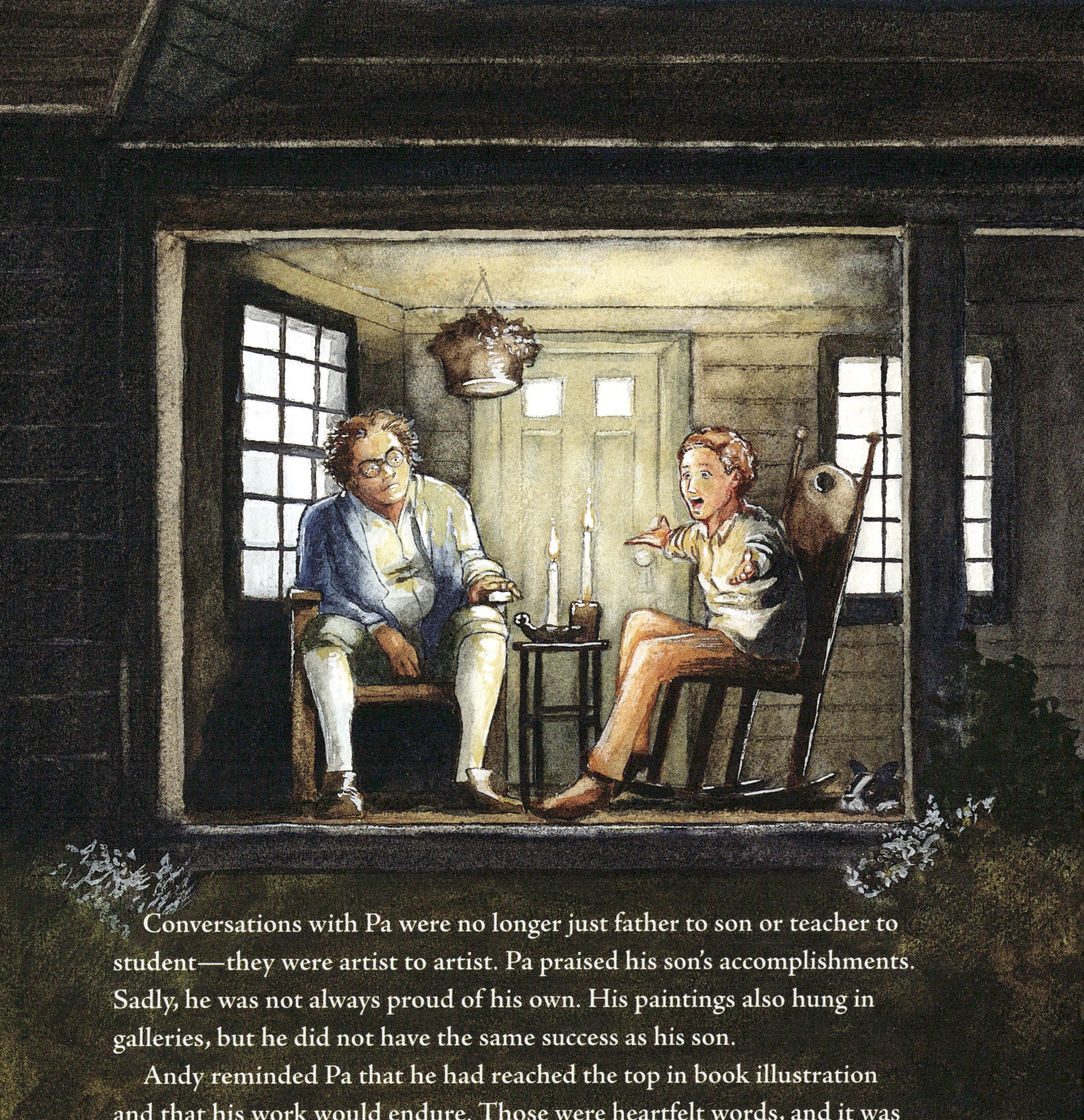

Conversations with Pa were no longer just father to son or teacher to student—they were artist to artist. Pa praised his son's accomplishments. Sadly, he was not always proud of his own. His paintings also hung in galleries, but he did not have the same success as his son.

Andy reminded Pa that he had reached the top in book illustration and that his work would endure. Those were heartfelt words, and it was the right time to say them.

October 19, 1945, was a life-changing day.

Andy got a call that shattered his world. There was a horrible accident. Pa was driving with his grandson Newell. The local railroad tracks had no warning signals or safety gates at the crossing. The train was not able to stop in time to save their lives.

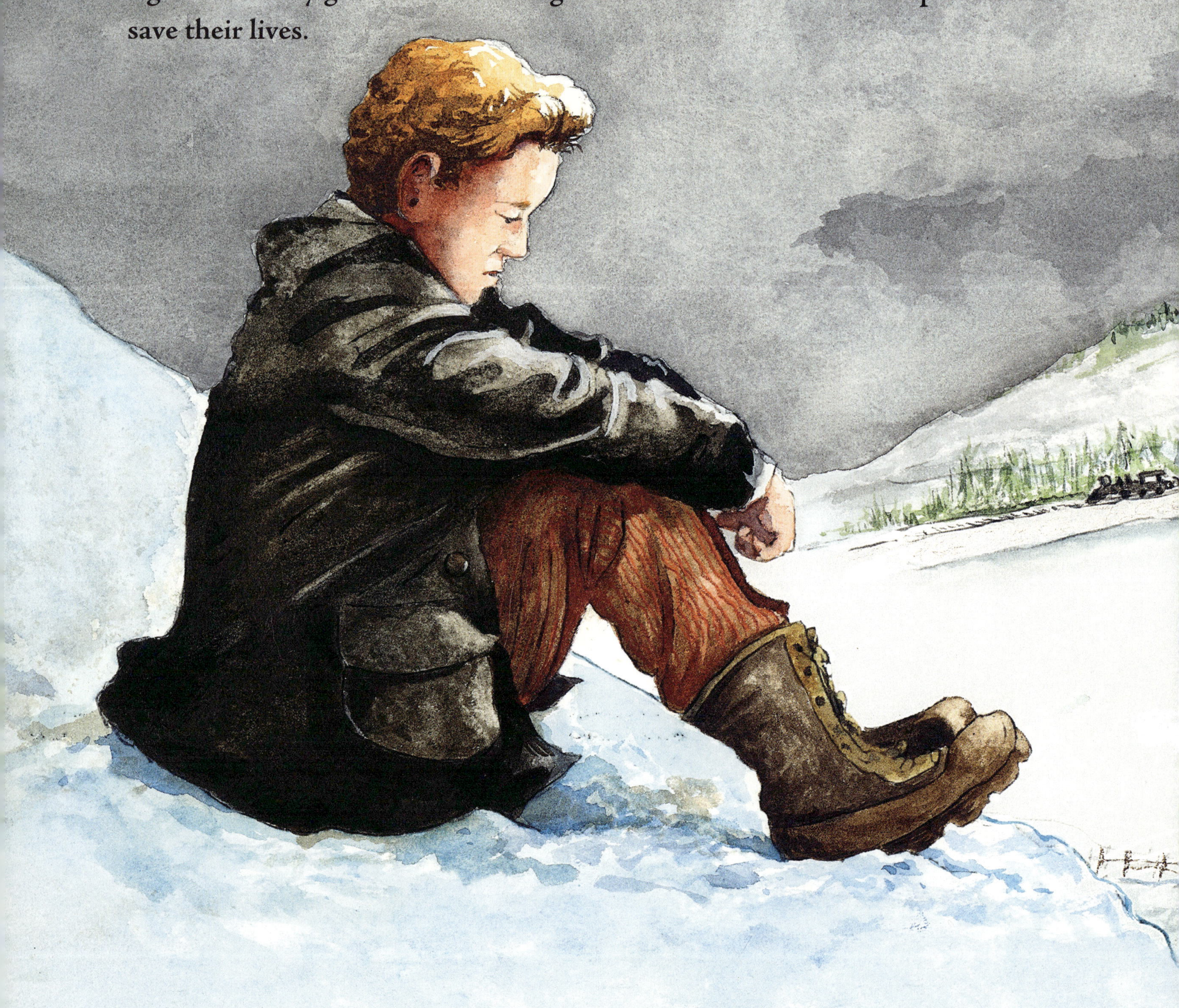

Andy lost his father, his teacher, and his friend. He was devastated. The only way to comfort himself was to paint.

"I had always had this great emotion toward the landscape, and so, with his death . . . the landscape took on a meaning—the quality of him," Andy said of his father. "His death really gave me a meaning to paint."

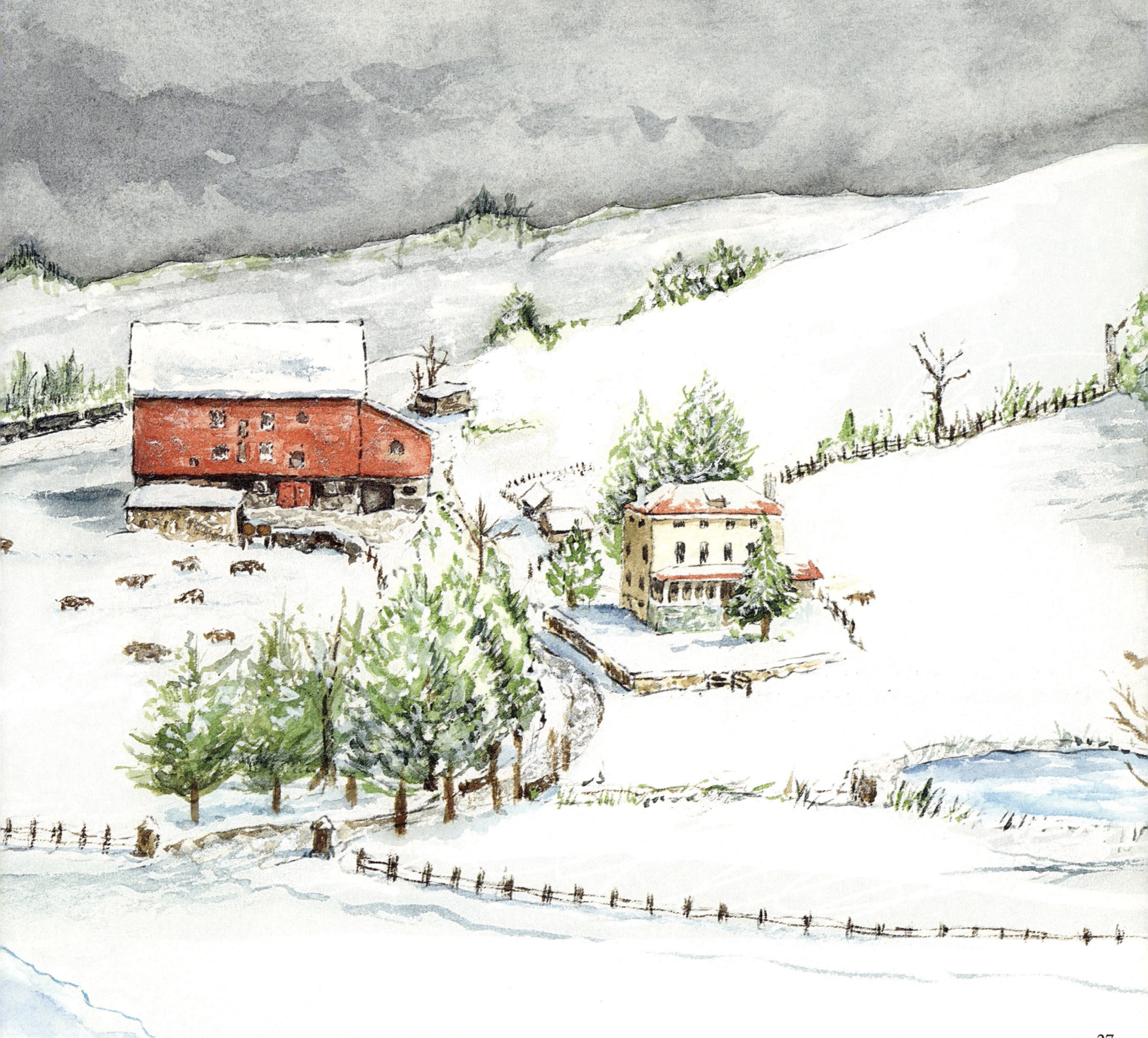

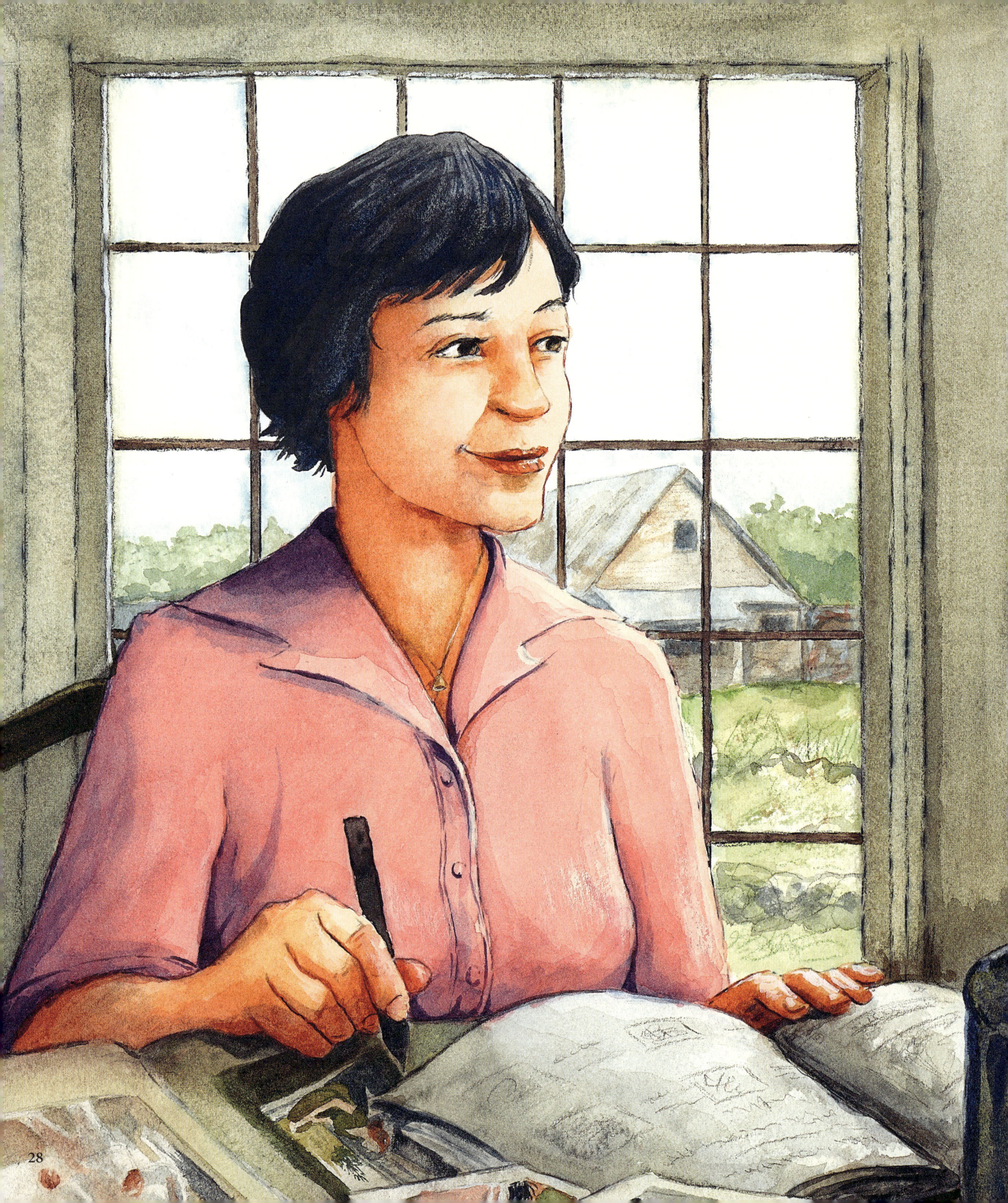

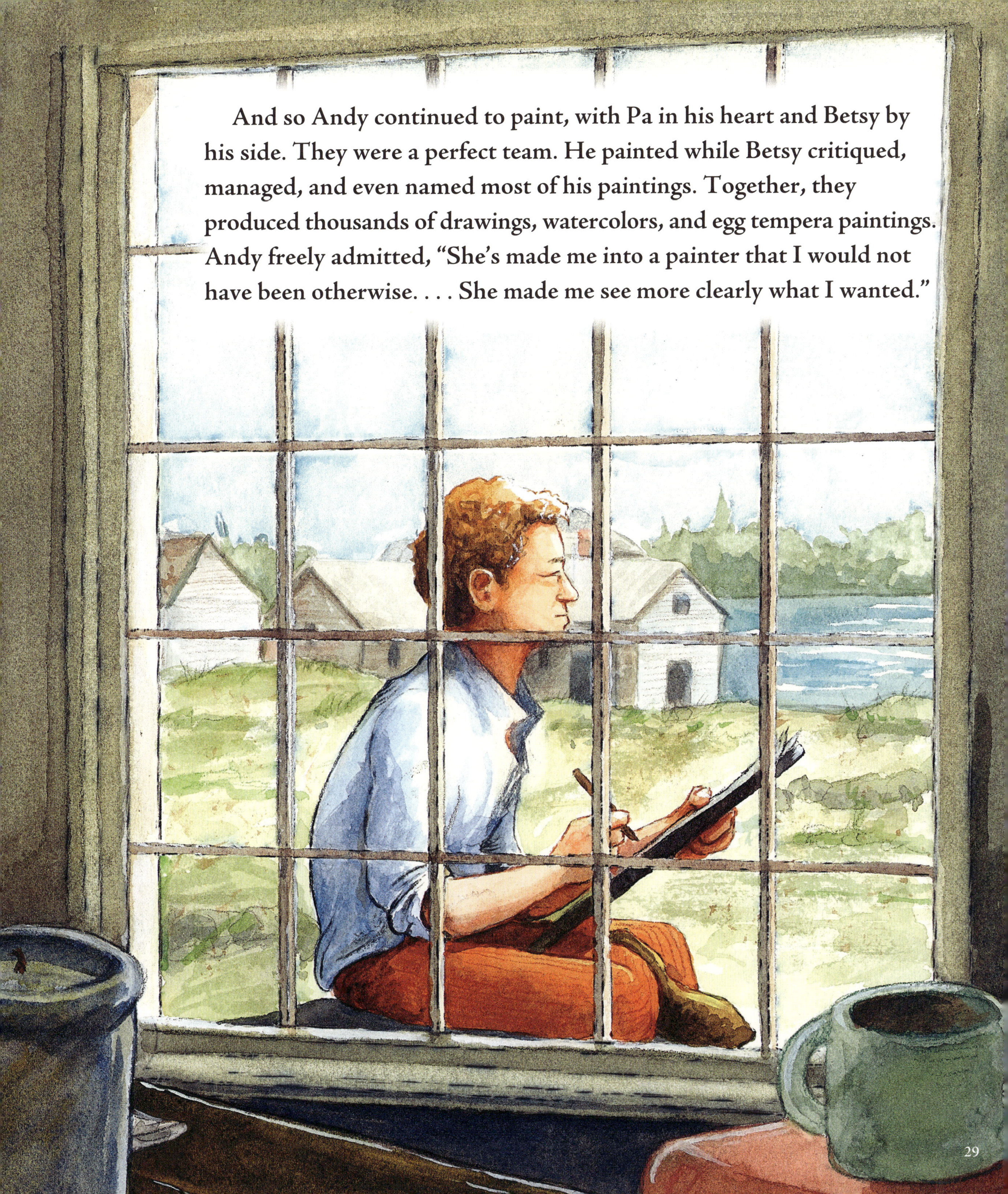

And so Andy continued to paint, with Pa in his heart and Betsy by his side. They were a perfect team. He painted while Betsy critiqued, managed, and even named most of his paintings. Together, they produced thousands of drawings, watercolors, and egg tempera paintings. Andy freely admitted, "She's made me into a painter that I would not have been otherwise. . . . She made me see more clearly what I wanted."

The paintings tell Andy and Betsy's life story in the same ways that diaries and scrapbooks do; the people and places were an intimate part of their lives. New buds on a tree in spring. A friend's face changing over decades. The frail texture of a worn blouse. A spectrum of colors visible on a young girl's cheek. Crumbling walls that hold memories.

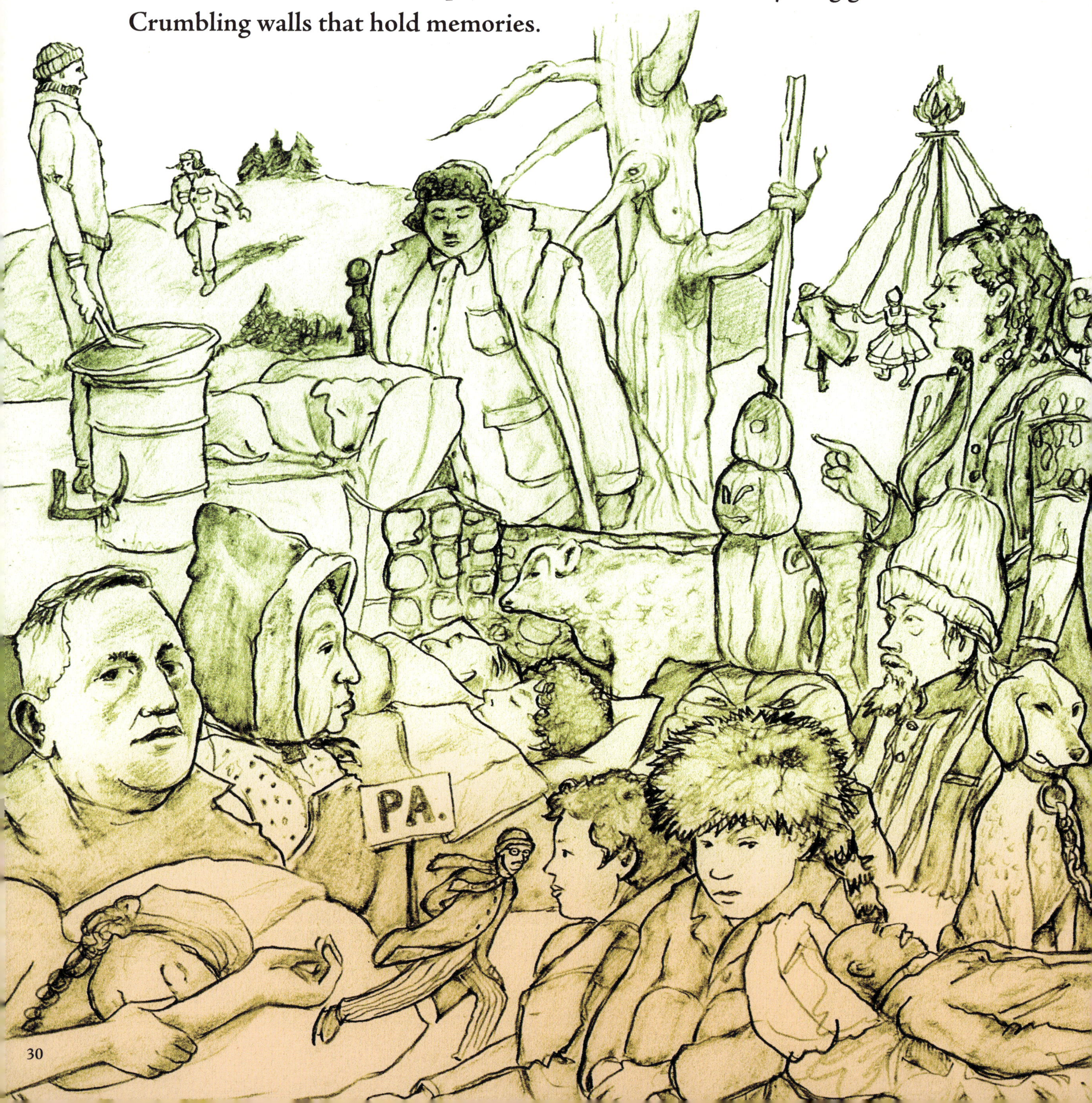

Andy's watercolors can be abstract and wild. As if his brush cut across the paper like a sword, splashing paint in every direction. The egg temperas can feel quiet and poetic, carefully crafted in a private meditation over the course of months.

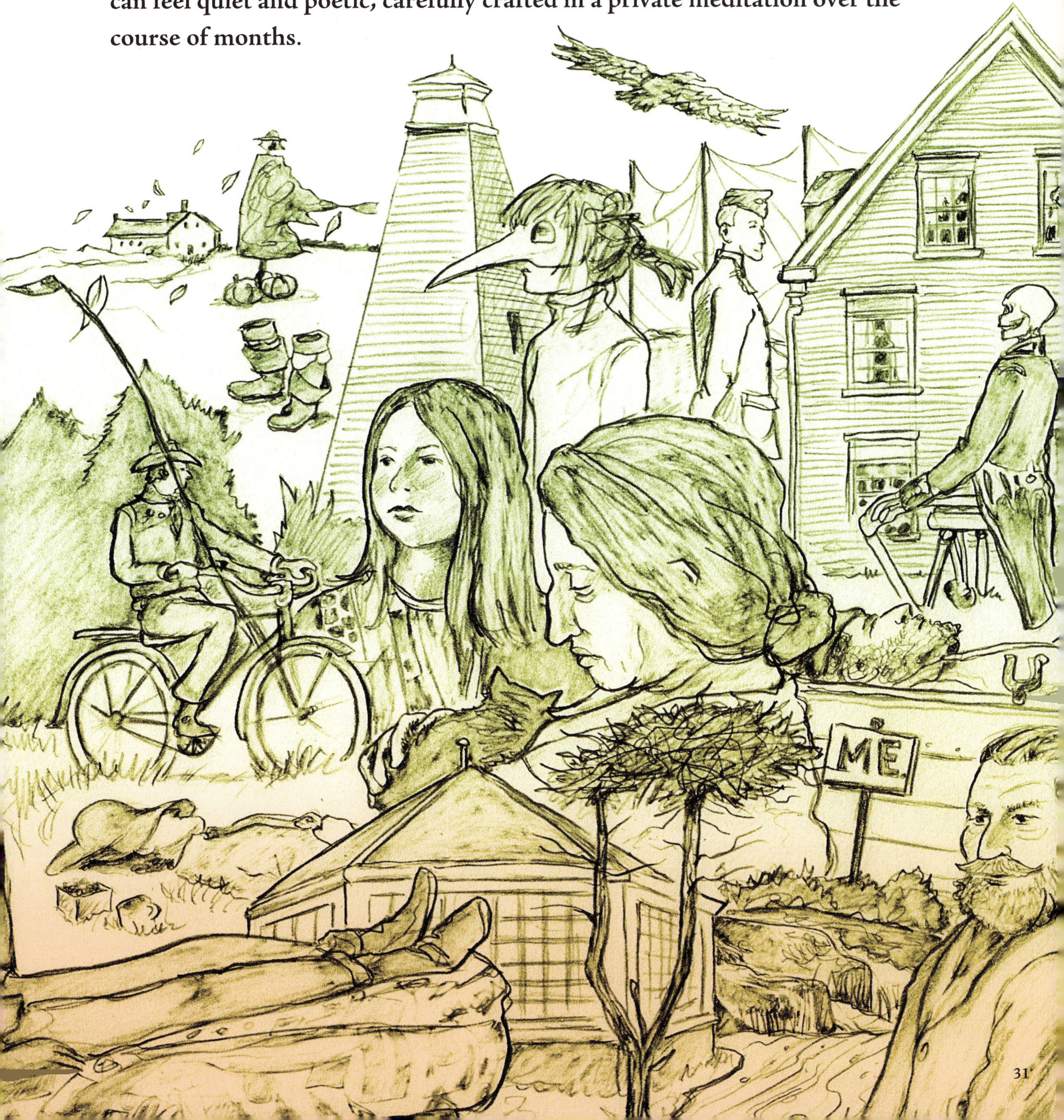

Andrew Wyeth is remembered as one of the great American painters of the twentieth century, and his popularity continues to grow and inspire young artists.

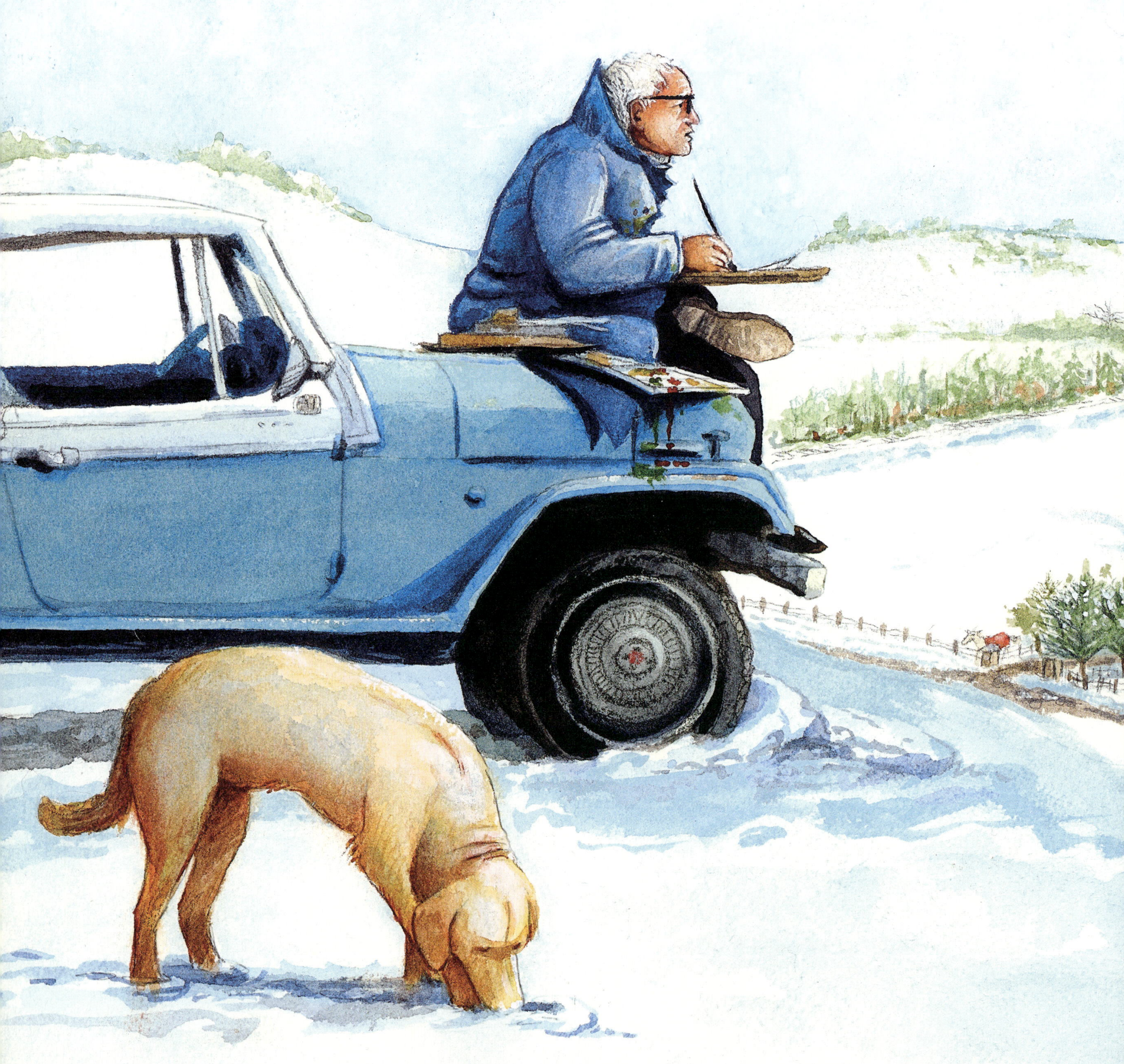

Throughout his life, as his paintings traveled to be seen in galleries and museums across the globe, Andy usually stayed put. The reason was simple: He didn't want to miss a single day of painting.

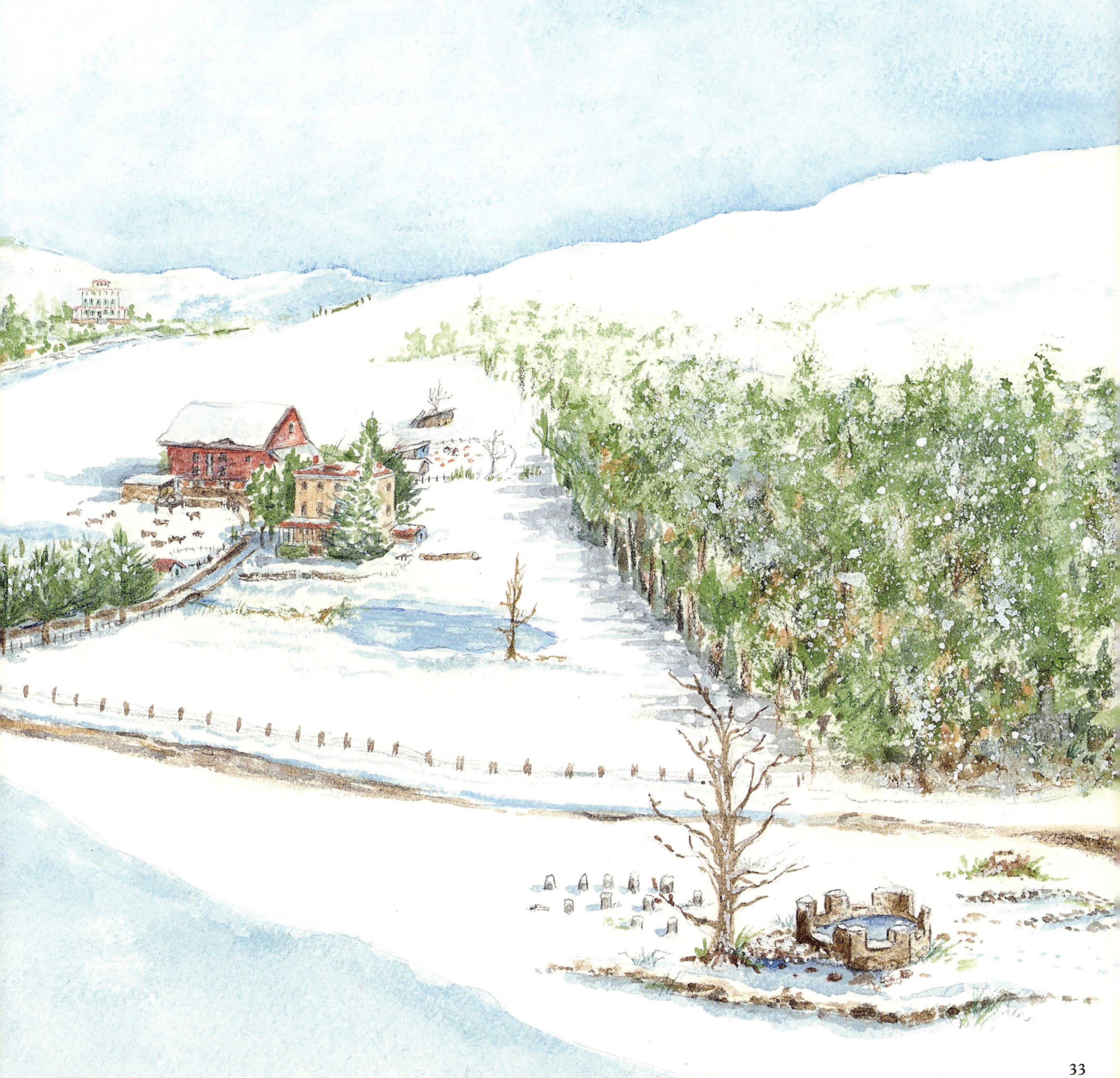

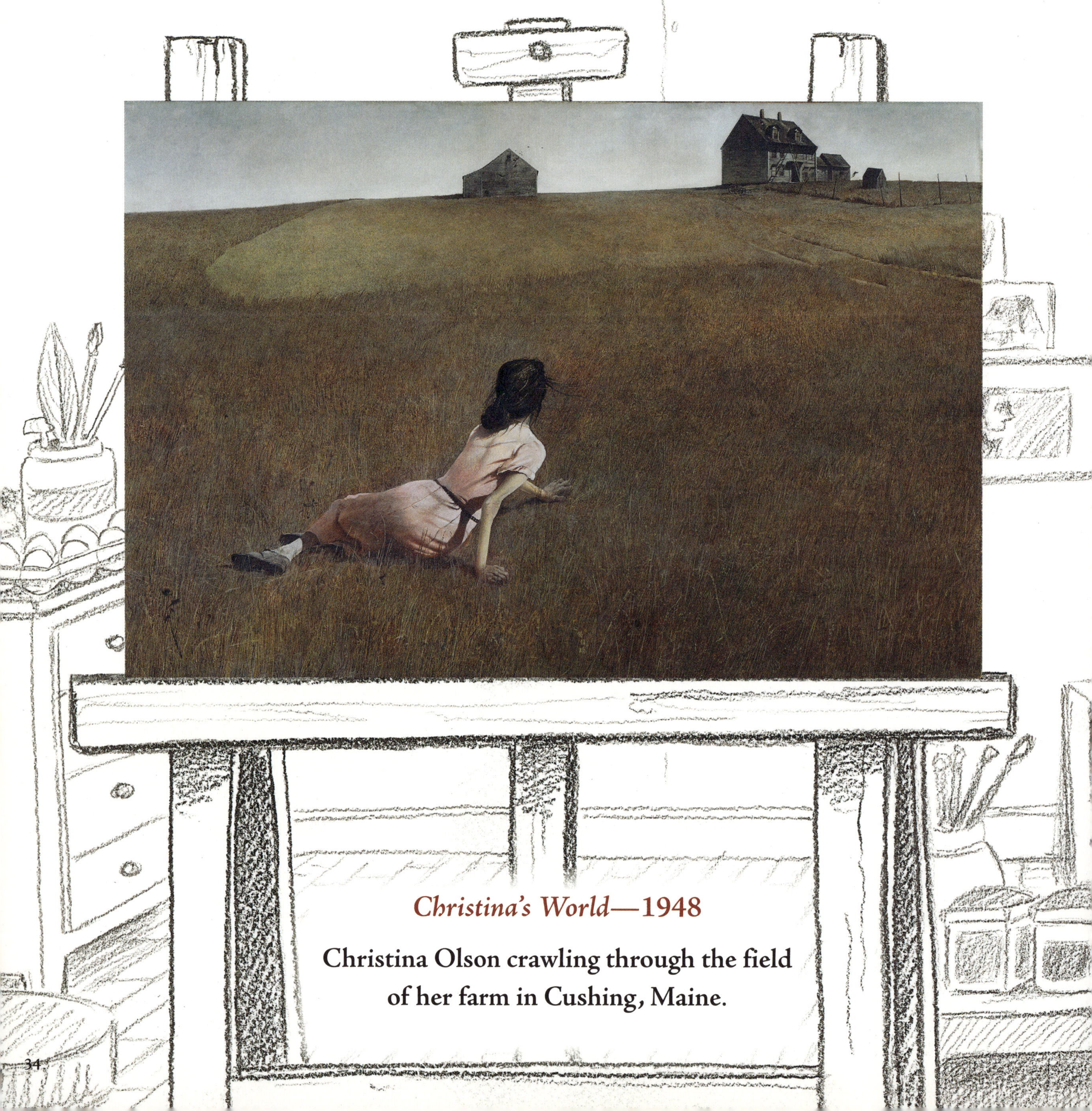

Christina's World—1948

**Christina Olson crawling through the field
of her farm in Cushing, Maine.**

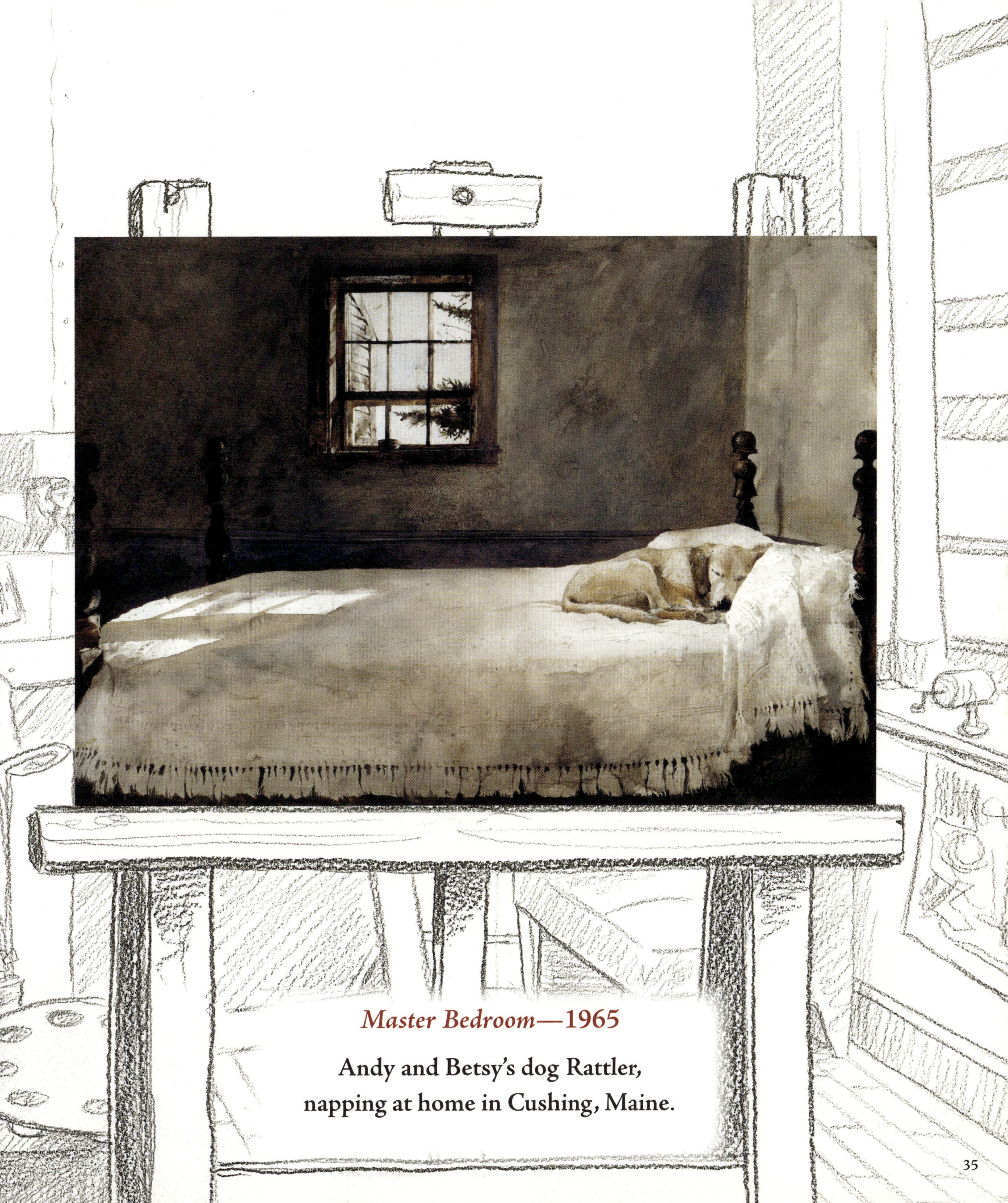

Master Bedroom—1965

Andy and Betsy's dog Rattler,
napping at home in Cushing, Maine.

Several of Andy's favorite Pennsylvania models dancing
around the maypole.

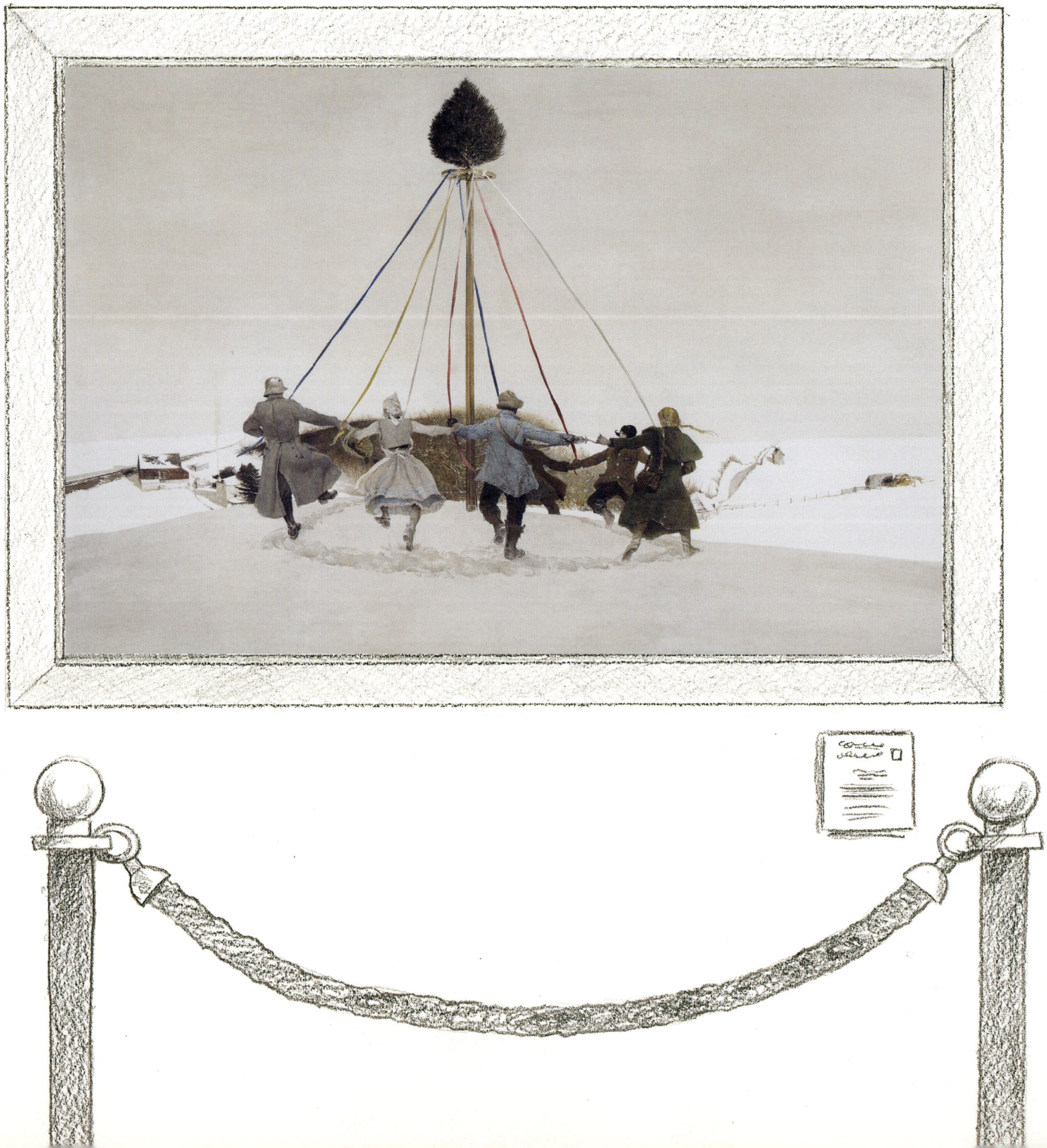

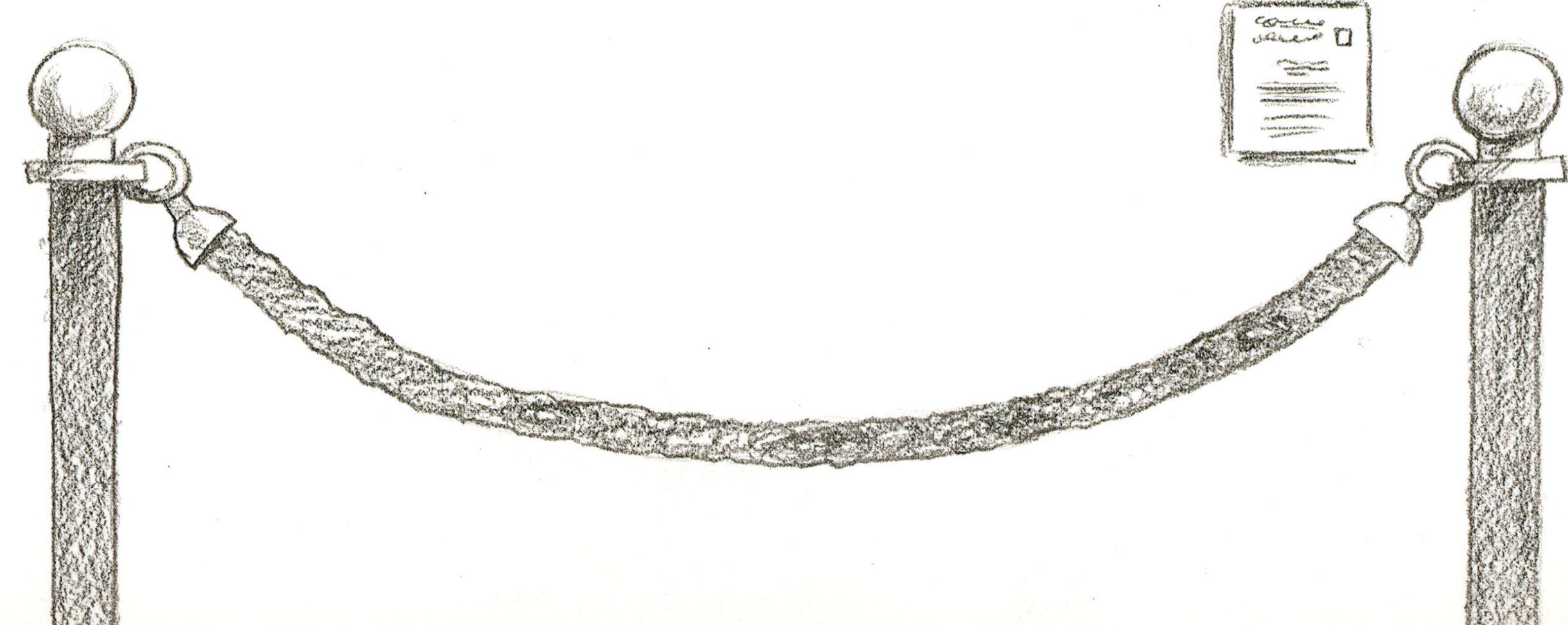

The Carry—2003

This painting is of Goose River, in Waldoboro, Maine.

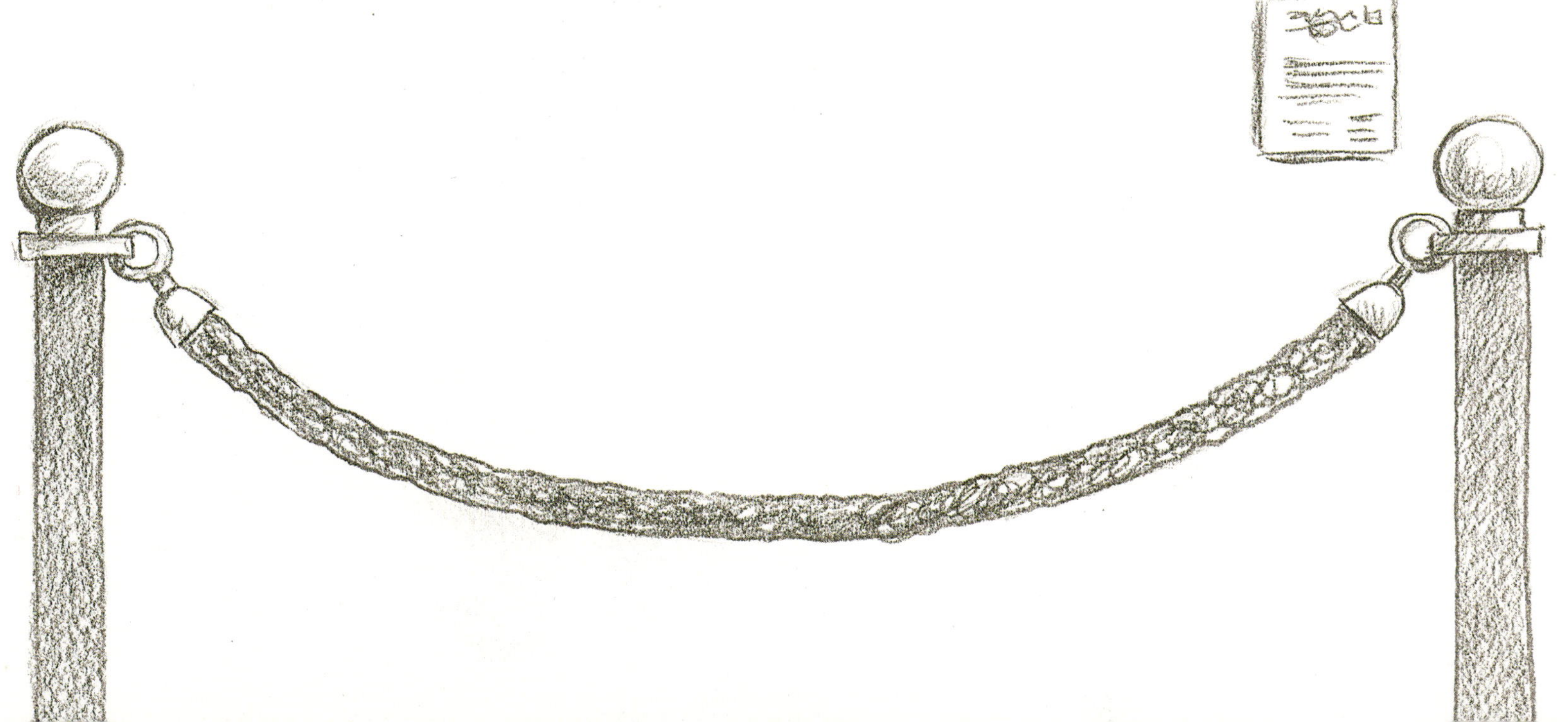

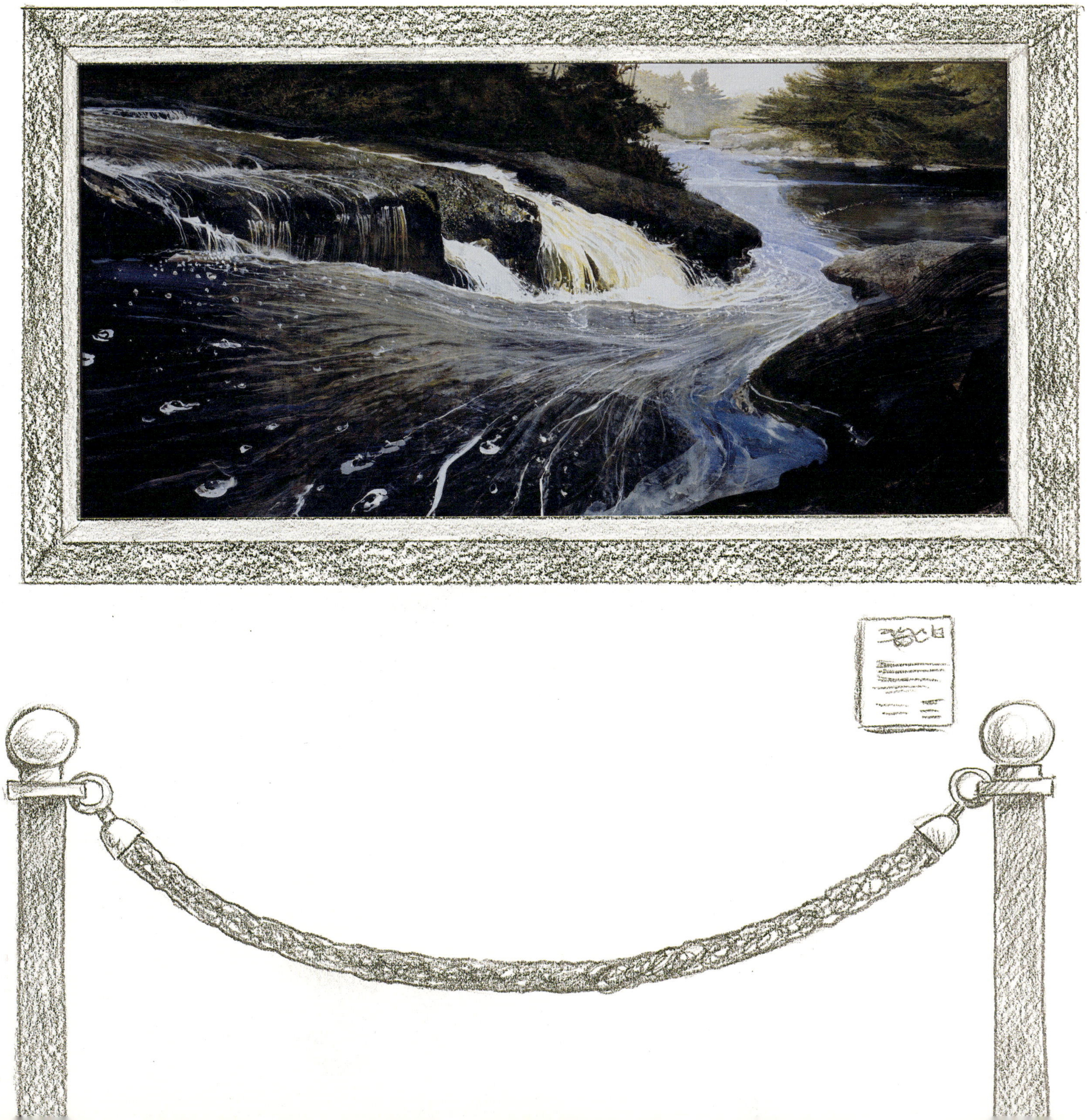

Andy's sisters Henriette and Carolyn became accomplished painters. His brother, Nathaniel, focused his creativity on engineering and patented twenty-five products. His sister Ann was a pianist and composer. Several of her compositions were performed by the Philadelphia Orchestra.

Andy and Betsy raised two sons. Nicholas became an art dealer, and Jamie became an acclaimed painter, which is not surprising, since their childhoods were filled with imagination and creativity. Much like N.C. had done for Andy all those years earlier. Andy and Betsy's final resting place is on Christina Olson's farm, where they spent their very first day together.

Quotes by Andrew Wyeth

❧

"I think one's art goes as far and as deep as one's love goes."

❧

"I'm supersensitive. Some little thing can ruin my whole day. But you've got to be vulnerable. Otherwise, you're no good. Keep your spirit open. That's the whole thing."

❧

"I'm really painting my own life."

Four Favorite Art Techniques of Andrew Wyeth's

Pencil: For preliminary studies on a subject. He added notes about form, texture, color, and more.

Watercolor: He painted with it quickly, to capture his initial spark of inspiration.

Drybrush: To add sharper detail to his watercolor painting, he dipped his brush in watercolor paint, then squeezed out the excess water with his fingers to paint drier and bolder lines.

Egg tempera: A lengthy process of building up layers of paint to get a desired texture and blend of colors. Andy liked this process because it gave him more time to live with his paintings and subjects.

Did You Know?

- As a child, Andy would pull Pa's illustrations out of storage and ask him to explain the stories inside them.

- Andy had hundreds of toy soldiers. He made up stories for all of them and could remember their names even as an adult.

- Andy learned how to use egg tempera paint from one of N.C.'s students, Peter Hurd, who later married Andy's sister Henriette. His sister Ann married another student of N.C.'s, named John McCoy. And both of N.C.'s sons married daughters of painters.

- Andy never painted from photographs. He painted from life or from memory.

- Close friends let Andy wander freely in and around their homes, day or night, to paint whenever he was inspired.

- Andy wished that he could be invisible, or just be a pair of eyes, so he could capture people in their most natural moments.

- Andy never felt the need to change his style to fit in with popular trends. That made him unpopular with certain critics who failed to see that his realistic subjects were depicted with modern, abstract compositions and painting techniques.

- Eventually, Andy wanted the freedom to create paintings without being critiqued, so for fifteen years, he painted a model named Helga and didn't share them with anyone.

- During Andy's final days, in 2009, a friend witnessed a beautiful moment as he slept. His hand was moving back and forth, as if he were holding a paintbrush.

- All the images on pages 30–31 are details from the following paintings by Andrew Wyeth: *A Winter Day on the Brandywine* (1940); *Soaring* (1942–1950); *Winter 1946* (1946); *Young America* (1950); *Faraway* (1952); *Miss Olson* (1952); *Karl* (1954); *Untitled* (Osprey nest in a tree, 1954); *Lifeboat House* (1954); *Nicholas* (1955); *Roasted Chestnuts* (1956); *Raccoon* (1958); *Young Bull* (1960); *Distant Thunder* (1961); *Garret Room* (1962); *Adam* (1963); *V.F.W.* (study, 1964); *Master Bedroom* (1965); *Weatherside* (1965); *Siri* (1970); *Sea Dog* (1971); *Witch Country, Cushing* (1973); *Jack-Be-Nimble* (1976); *Sea Boots* (1976); *Night Cap* (1978); *Day Dream* (1980); *Dr. Syn* (1981); *Adrift* (1982); *Winter Carnival* (1985); *Pentecost* (1989); *Snow Hill* (1989); *Marriage* (1993); *Two If by Sea* (1995); *Airborne* (1996); *Merlin* (1998); *Guest Room* (1998); *Walking Stick* (2002); *The Carry* (2003).

Bibliography

Books

Wyeth, Andrew, and Richard Meryman. *Andrew Wyeth: A Spoken Self-Portrait*. National Gallery of Art, Washington. D.A.P., 2013.

Wyeth, Andrew, and Thomas Hoving. *Andrew Wyeth: Autobiography*. Bulfinch Press, 1980.

Wyeth, N. C. *The Wyeths: The Letters of N. C. Wyeth, 1901–1945*. Edited by Betsy James Wyeth. Gambit, 1970.

Films

Bartlett, Bo, dir. *Andrew Wyeth–Self Portrait: Snow Hill*. Produced by Betsy James Wyeth. Chip Taylor Communications, 1995.

Holsten, Glenn, dir. *Wyeth: American Masters*. Produced by Chayne Gregg. PBS, 2018.

Snell, Andrew, dir. *Andrew Wyeth*. Films for the Humanities, 1980. https://www.youtube.com/watch?v=GppHUk9fPIs&t=5s.

Paintings Reproduced in the Book

All Andrew Wyeth artwork: © 2025 Wyeth Foundation for American Art/Artists Society (ARS) New York.

Page 7: Wyeth, N. C. *The Wild, Spectacular Race for Dinner*. 1905. Oil on canvas, 38⅛" x 26" (96.8 x 66 cm). Buffalo Bill Historical Center, Cody, Wyoming. Gift of John M. Schiff, 44.83.

Page 21: Wyeth, Andrew. *The Lobsterman*. 1937. Watercolor on paper, 21½" x 29" (54.6 x 73.7 cm). Hunter Museum of American Art. Chattanooga, Tennessee. Gift of Benwood Foundation.

Page 34: Wyeth, Andrew. *Christina's World*. 1948. Tempera on panel, 32¼" x 47¾" (81.9 x 121.3 cm). Museum of Modern Art, New York.

Page 35: Wyeth, Andrew. *Master Bedroom*. 1965. Watercolor on paper, 21⅛" x 29½" (53.7 x 74.9 cm). Private collection.

Page 36: Wyeth, Andrew. *Snow Hill*. 1989. Tempera on panel, 48" x 72" (121.9 x 182.9 cm). Wyeth Foundation for American Art.

Page 37: Wyeth, Andrew. *The Carry*. 2003. Tempera on panel, 24" x 48" (61 x 121.9 cm). Private collection.

Quote Sources

11 "Andy, you know, we must be like a sponge": *The Wyeths: A Father and His Family*, Smithsonian World, directed by David Grubin, aired November 24, 1986, https://www.youtube.com/watch?v=fjwGL2rrWKE.

21 "At last, a man who has the guts to present nature honestly": Wyeth, *The Wyeths*, 768.

22 "I knew at some point somebody was going to find me": Richard Meryman, *Andrew Wyeth: A Secret Life* (New York: HarperCollins, 1996), 151.

24 "Well, then you better marry her": Victoria Wyeth, "Thoughts on Paper," Virtual Gallery Talk with the Brandywine Museum of Art, May 24, 2022.

27 "I had always had this great emotion toward the landscape": *Wyeth*, Glenn Holsten.

27 "His death really gave me a meaning to paint": *Andrew Wyeth*, Andrew Snell.

29 "She's made me into a painter": Andrew Wyeth to his biographer, Richard Meryman, in 1966.

38 "I think one's art goes as far and as deep": Richard Meryman, "Andrew Wyeth and His Art: America's Pre-Eminent Painter Relates a Unique Chronicle of a Work of Art," *Life*, May 14, 1965.

38 "I'm supersensitive": Richard Meryman, *Andrew Wyeth: First Impressions* (New York: Harry N. Abrams, Inc., 1991), 44.

38 "I'm really painting my own life": *Wyeth*, Glenn Holsten.

For Benjamin. Soak it all up, my son.

This book has brought many new friends into my life, and they could not have been more generous with the resources, stories, and experiences they provided me. Some of them were Andrew and Betsy Wyeth's dear friends and loved ones: Victoria Browning Wyeth, Mary Landa, Karen Baumgartner, Jim Duff, and Karl J. Kuerner. Some of them keep the Wyeth legacy alive through the Brandywine Museum of Art: Will Coleman, Mary Cronin, Wawa Ingersoll, Lillian Kinney, Christine Podmaniczky, Liesl Mahoney, and Laura Westmoreland. Some are my not-so-new friends: Glenn Holsten, John Desiderio, Stuart Reeves, and Adam Potkay. Finally, the Christian C. Sanderson Museum—where this book was first inspired.

ABOUT THIS BOOK

The illustrations for this book were done in watercolor and colored pencil on Arches cold-press 140-lb. watercolor paper. This book was edited by Christy Ottaviano and designed by Tracy Shaw. The production was supervised by Lillian Sun, and the production editor was Jen Graham. The text and display type were set in Jenson Pro.